God and Alcoholism

Other Titles by Dick B.

Dr. Bob and His Library: Books for Twelve Step Growth
Anne Smith's Journal, 1933-1939: A.A.'s Principles of Success
The Oxford Group and Alcoholics Anonymous
    A Design for Living That Works
The Akron Genesis of Alcoholics Anonymous
New Light on Alcoholism: God, Sam Shoemaker, and A.A.
The Books Early AAs Read for Spiritual Growth
Courage to Change (with Bill Pittman)
The Good Book and The Big Book: A.A.'s Roots in the Bible
That Amazing Grace
    The Role of Clarence and Grace S. in Alcoholics Anonymous
Good Morning!
    Quiet Time, Morning Watch, Meditation, and Early A.A.
Turning Point
    A History of Early A.A.'s Spiritual Roots and Successes
Utilizing Early A.A.'s Spiritual Roots for Recovery Today
The Golden Text of A.A.: God, the Pioneers, and Real Spirituality
By the Power of God
    A Guide to Early A.A. Groups & Forming Similar Groups Today
Making Known the Biblical History and Roots of Alcoholics Anonymous
    An Eleven-Year Research, Writing, Publishing, and Fact
    Dissemination Project
Why Early A.A. Succeeded
    The Good Book in Alcoholics Anonymous Yesterday and Today
    (A Bible Study Primer for AAs and other 12-Steppers)

God and Alcoholism

Our Growing Opportunity in the 21ˢᵗ Century

Dick B.

Paradise Research Publications, Inc.
Kihei, Maui, Hawaii

Paradise Research Publications, Inc., P.O. Box 837, Kihei, HI
96753-0837

This Paradise Research Publications Edition is published by
arrangement with Good Book Publishing Company, P.O. Box 837,
Kihei, Maui, HI 96753-0837

The publication of this volume does not imply affiliation with nor
approval or endorsement from Alcoholics Anonymous World
Services, Inc. The views expressed herein are solely those of the
author. A.A. is a program of recovery from alcoholism–use of the
Twelve Steps in connection with programs and activities which are
patterned after A.A., but which address other problems, does not
imply otherwise.

Publisher's Cataloguing-in-Publication
(Provided by Quality Books, Inc.)

B., Dick. ___
    God and alcoholism : our growing opportunity in the
21st century / by Dick B. – 1st ed.
    p. cm.
    Includes bibliographical references and index.
    ISBN 1-885803-34-6

    1. Alcoholics–Rehabilitation. 2. Alcoholics–
Rehabilitation–Biblical teaching. 3. Recovering
alcoholics–Religious life. 4. Alcoholics Anonymous–
History. 5. Behavior modification. 6. God. I. Title

HV5275.B13 2002   362.292'86
                        QBI02-701522

Contents

1

The Real Facts about
A.A.'s Pioneer Group

A New Spiritual Recovery Program with
Enormous Potential

Writings abound today about: whether A.A. does or does not work; what its success rate is or isn't; what its success rate at the beginning was or wasn't; whether A.A. is or was religious or spiritual; whether alcoholism is or is not a sin or a disease; what a "higher power" is or isn't; whether A.A. is or was about God or merely about anything you might want to call a god; and about what can truly and accurately be called the real "basics" of A.A.

But I have believed and believe, and have researched and found, that the first group in A.A.–Akron Number One, as Bill Wilson called it–provides the proper starting point for a look at A.A., its roots, its history, its nature, its successes, and its God–the Creator. The first group did in fact have its share of alcoholics who wandered by; but the "real" alcoholics who "really tried" (as Bill Wilson described them) were a sturdy band of "last gasp" alcoholics who had stayed sober for about two years since A.A.'s founding days of 1935. This bunch were called the "Pioneers." Their group–the first actual group in and of Alcoholics Anonymous–was the "self-styled Alcoholic Group of Akron, Ohio." Their leader, Dr. Robert Holbrook Smith ("Dr. Bob"), called them a Christian Fellowship. And they numbered some forty in all.

This Pioneer Group, with their astonishing success rate of at least seventy-five percent among "medically incurable" alcoholics, developed–from religion, medicine, and their own experience–the basic

1

ideas and spiritual program of Alcoholics Anonymous. And it was that *new* spiritual program of recovery, founded on reliance on God, that gave great promise to America and the world.

Whether right or wrong, psychiatrist and writer M. Scott Peck stated (and is often quoted for the following evaluation by him), in *Further Along the Road Less Traveled*:

> I believe the greatest positive event of the twentieth century occurred in Akron, Ohio. . . . when Bill W. and Dr. Bob convened the first Alcoholics Anonymous meeting. It was not only the beginning of the self-help movement and the beginning of the integration of science and spirituality at a grass-roots level, but also the beginning of the community movement . . . which is going to be the salvation not only of alcoholics and addicts but of us all (Howard Clinebell, Ph.D. *Understanding and Counseling Persons with Alcohol, Drug, and Behavioral Addictions* [Nashville: Abingdon Press, 1998], p. 196).

The Frank Amos Reports on A.A.'s Pioneer Group (Akron Number One) Program

After locating and analyzing a number of different statements as to the actual program of A.A.'s founding years, I discovered that most of the statements were either inaccurate, incomplete, or mistaken as to the dates involved; or they were or just plain, dead wrong. In the earlier years of research, my focus was on the *roots* of the program, rather than on the *ingredients* of the Pioneer program. Finally, I realized that Bill Wilson himself had put in motion an investigation in 1938 of just what *was* going on in Akron in the 1930's, and just what the program in Akron really involved. That investigation culminated in two reports by John D. Rockefeller, Jr.'s associate Frank Amos. And the reports were made, in part even before A.A.'s Big Book was commenced, and substantially before that "basic text" was published in the Spring of 1939. The specificity and accuracy of the Amos reports assures us of their great importance today.

How These Historically Important Reports by Frank Amos Came About

Bill Wilson recorded that, in November, 1937, he and Dr. Bob sat in the living room of Dr. Bob's home in Akron counting recoveries. Wilson said: "A hard core of very grim, last-gasp cases had by then been sober a couple of years. All told, we figured that upwards of 40 alcoholics were staying bone dry, and Bob and Anne [Bob's wife] and I bowed our heads in silent thanks." Bill began to think of setting up a chain of profit-making hospitals, of raising money, of subsidizing missionaries, and of writing a book of experiences that would carry *the* message of recovery to other cities and other countries. Dr. Bob sided with Bill on the need for a book, but was "frankly dubious" about the hospitals, paid missionaries, and fund raising. Dr. Bob and Bill talked it over with the other members in Akron. There was a long, hard-fought session, but together, Bill and Bob persuaded a bare majority of 18 AAs gathered at T. Henry Williams's home in Akron to accept the whole package–book, hospitals, missionaries, and fund raising. Wilson returned to New York "to try to raise the millions that would be needed." Meanwhile, Dr. Bob was investigating possibilities for a hospital in Akron. (*DR. BOB and the Good Oldtimers* [New York: Alcoholics Anonymous World Services, 1980], pp. 123-24, 128).

In New York, Bill got to see John D. Rockefeller, Jr. And Rockefeller dispatched Frank Amos out to Akron to investigate what was going on. (Amos was soon to become one of A.A.'s first non-alcoholic trustees.) Amos carried out his job thoroughly–investigating what he called the "self-styled Alcoholic Group of Akron, Ohio." Amos called on Dr. Bob and attended meetings. He questioned members and nonmembers, including professional associates of Dr. Bob. These included an eye specialist (Dr. Ferguson) and a general practitioner (Dr. Howard S.) who had been "an alcoholic and had been **cured** by Smith and his friends' activities and the Christian technique prescribed." Amos interviewed a retired judge who was chairman of the board of Akron City Hospital. He also met with a number of men, their wives, and some of their mothers, hearing stories–"many of them almost miraculous" (*DR. BOB and the Good Oldtimers*, pp. 128-30; bold face added). Amos then, as the result of his February, 1938, investigation, spelled out the Akron program in precise and simple terms we shall quote in a moment. He also suggested that Rockefeller donate $50,000.00 to the movement. However, Albert Scott, one of Rockefeller's advisers and also chairman of the board of trustees of New York's Riverside Church, argued the same point that had been argued by the minority in the Akron meeting at the Williams home–that money, property, and professionalism might "spoil this thing" (*DR. BOB and the Good Oldtimers*, pp. 134-35).

Amos rendered another "pre-Big Book" report later in 1938. He said that, by then, there were 110 members in the program, of whom 70 were in the Akron-Cleveland area. He observed: ". . . in many respects, their meetings have taken on the form of the meetings described in the Gospels [*sic*] of the early Christians during the first century." Regrettably for A.A., I believe, the writer of A.A.'s official biography of Dr. Bob Smith (*DR. BOB and the Good Oldtimers)* then gratuitously added the following statement–which was not at all a part of the Amos report: "It might also be noted that many terms now considered by A.A.'s to be misleading were then used, not only by non-A.A.'s discussing the movement, but sometimes by members themselves: 'cure,' 'ex-alcoholic,' 'reformed alcoholic'" (*DR. BOB and the Good Oldtimers*, pp. 135-36). But, in my own view, the writer's taking of such "editorial" liberty amounted to a flat statement that the founding fathers and Rockefeller's own people, in talking about a "cure," were using "misleading" terms in their early statements and work. And therein lies one of the several reasons for my very presentation in this particular day.

The Amos reports were made available to me by A.A.'s archivist at General Services in New York and also by the Stepping Stones archivist in Bedford Hills, New York. I hasten to point out that the idea of "cure" was *not* considered "misleading" by the founders who experienced and witnessed the cures. They explicitly and repeatedly called them "cures." We soon will cover some of their actual statements to that effect. But it is highly significant that Bill Wilson (who can and should be called A.A. Number One) and Bill Dotson (A.A. Number Three) both made it clear they had been "cured" of alcoholism. Dr. Bob used the same term when contacting his own professionals. The "cure" statements of all three AAs are often quoted in A.A. Conference Approved literature–even in A.A.'s new "Fourth Edition," published in 2001. Thus both Bill Wilson and Bill Dotson are quoted as saying: "The Lord has been so wonderful to me, **curing** me of this terrible disease, that I just want to keep telling people about it" (*Alcoholics Anonymous*, 4th ed., p. 191; bold face added).

The Precise Details about the Pioneer Group Program–As Reported by Frank Amos

Amos stated to Rockefeller, as to the alcoholic group he had investigated, that the alcoholics were "all considered practically incurable by physicians." He said they had "been reformed and so far have remained teetotalers." As to their stories, he noted that, when it came to recovery, the stories were all remarkably alike in "the technique used and the system followed." He detailed their "Program" as follows (See *DR. BOB and the Good Oldtimers*, pp. 130-31):

1. An alcoholic must realize that he is an alcoholic, incurable from a medical viewpoint, and that he must never again drink anything with alcohol in it.

2. He must surrender himself absolutely to God, realizing that in himself there is no hope.

3. Not only must he want to stop drinking permanently, he must remove from his life other sins such as hatred, adultery, and others which frequently accompany alcoholism. Unless he will do this absolutely, Smith and his associates refuse to work with him.

4. He must have devotions every morning–a "quiet time" of prayer and some reading from the Bible and other religious literature. Unless this is faithfully followed, there is grave danger of backsliding.

5. He must be willing to help other alcoholics get straightened out. This throws up a protective barrier and strengthens his own willpower and convictions.

6. It is important, but not vital, that he meet frequently with other reformed alcoholics and form both a social and a religious comradeship.

7. Important, but not vital, that he attend some religious service at least once weekly.

The Frank Amos reports also specifically added:

> The A.A. members of that time did not consider meetings necessary to maintain sobriety. They were simply "desirable." Morning devotion and "quiet time," however, were musts (*DR. BOB and the Good Oldtimers*, p. 136).

The "Musts" of the Pioneers' Program

The seven points of the Pioneer program as described by Frank Amos can appropriately be supplemented by also recalling several commonly stated and well-documented "musts" the Pioneers considered essential *to* their seven-point "Program":

Complete Abstinence

Complete abstinence was a *must*. (*DR. BOB and the Good Oldtimers*, p. 131.)

Hospitalization

Hospitalization was another *must* in the early days. (*DR. BOB*, p. 102.)

"Surrender"

"Surrender" was a *must* (*DR. BOB*, pp. 101, 13). One detailed description and version of the "surrenders" mentioned below can be found in Mitchell K. *How It Worked: The Story of Clarence H. Snyder and the Early Days of Alcoholics Anonymous in Cleveland, Ohio* (NY: AA Big Book Study Group, 1997), pp. 58, 68-71; and, from several sources, the evidence about "surrender" strongly indicates it involved the following:

- At the hospital with Dr. Bob–accepting Christ and praying on your knees (*DR. BOB*, p. 118).

- Upstairs at T. Henry Williams's Home–"real" surrenders (*DR. BOB*, p. 101). Three different old-timers verified to my satisfaction their own born again experiences that took place. These men were Clarence Snyder, Ed Andy, and Larry Bauer (Dick B., *The Golden Text of A.A.: God, the Pioneers, and Real Spirituality.* [Kihei, HI: Paradise Research Publications, 2000], pp. 31-33; Mitchell K., *How It Worked*, p. 70). And the following were the elements of the surrenders that took place:

  - An "old fashioned prayer meeting" (*DR. BOB*, pp. 101, 139).

- Older members would pray for the newcomer and be guided by the language of James 5:13-16 (*DR. BOB*, p. 131). The "elders" would ask the newcomer to observe the Four Absolutes (Honesty, Purity, Unselfishness, and Love) and to help others who needed it (*DR. BOB*, p. 139). For a discussion of the origin and nature of the Four Absolutes, see Dick B., *The Oxford Group and Alcoholics Anonymous: A Design for Living That Works*. 2d ed., (Kihei, HI: Paradise Research Publications, 2000), pp. 237-46.

- The newcomer himself would then pray and surrender his life to God (accept Christ), also asking God to take alcohol out of his life (*DR. BOB*, p. 139).

Helping Others

Helping others was a *must*:

- "Our very lives, as ex-problem drinkers, depend upon our constant thought of others and how we may help meet their needs" (*Alcoholics Anonymous*, 4th ed., p. 20).

- "Faith without works is dead" (*Alcoholics Anonymous*, 4th ed., pp. 14, 76, 88).

Morning Devotion and Quiet Times

Morning devotions and Quiet Times were a *must*:

- Bible study, prayer, asking guidance, and religious reading were an integral part of Pioneer A.A. "quiet times" (*DR. BOB*, pp. 131, 150-51, 95-96).

- Studying the Sermon on the Mount, Book of James, and 1 Corinthians 13 was considered "absolutely essential" (*DR. BOB*, p. 96).

- Individual quiet times at home and during the day, as needed, were part of the process (*DR. BOB*, pp. 150-51).

Other Important, but Not "Essential," Parts of the Successful Program

- Morning quiet time with Anne Smith (Dr. Bob's wife) at the Smith home in Akron (prayer, Bible reading, guidance, discussions from Anne's Journal). See Dick B., *Anne Smith's Journal, 1933-1939*, 3rd ed., (Kihei HI: Paradise Research Publications, 1998).

- Personal time spent with Dr. Bob, Anne Smith, Henrietta Seiberling, and T. Henry Williams.

- Frequent fellowship with like-minded believers (social and religious).

- Meetings: Informal meetings occurred almost daily; there was also a set-up meeting on Monday; and a regular Oxford Group meeting on Wednesday, with prayer, Bible-reading, guidance, witnessing, topic discussion, surrenders, newcomer announcements, Lord's Prayer, and social time afterward for men and women (*DR. BOB*, p. 140). There were no drunkalogs.

- Religious reading recommended by Dr. Bob and Anne or circulated at meetings. (Dick B., *Dr. Bob and His Library*, 3rd ed. [Kihei, HI: Paradise Research Publications, 1998]; Dick B., *The Books Early AAs Read for Spiritual Growth*, 7th ed. [Kihei, HI: Paradise Research Publications, 1998];

Dick B., *Making Known the Biblical Roots of Alcoholics Anonymous: An Eleven Year Project*. [Kihei, HI: Paradise Research Publications, 2001]; Dick B., *Anne Smith's Journal, 1933-1939*).

- Affiliation with a church.

- An emphasis on family participation. This important element, involving participation by the entire family, has often been overlooked as to its early history and as to its existence in A.A. even today. It is not only documented, but Dr. Bob's kids and the Seiberling children have attested to this facet even in their recollections this very day. And the names of old timers and their wives are part of the original A.A. stories.

What Was *Not* Part of the Pioneer Group Program

- **No "Steps."** None! None at all. Not six. Not twelve. Nor did the Oxford Group have Steps.

- No focus by Akron Pioneers on Dr. Carl Jung's "conversion" prescription; no focus on Dr. Frank Buchman's much-discussed "spiritual experience" usages; and no special focus on the classic Oxford Group practice of "sharing for witness."

- No "world changing through life-changing" as in the Oxford Group and Moral Re-Armament (T. Willard Hunter. *World Changing Through Life Changing*. Thesis [Newton Center, Mass: Andover-Newton Theological School, 1977]).

- No central religious leader like Oxford Group founder Dr. Frank N. D. Buchman (Garth Lean. *On the Tail of a Comet: The Life of Frank Buchman*. [Colorado Springs: Helmers & Howard, 1988]).

- No "teams" sent around the U.S. and the world to change lives, leaders, and nations, as was regularly done by Dr. Buchman, by the Oxford Group, and by Moral Re-Armament (Frank N. D. Buchman. *Remaking the World.* [London: Blandford Press, 1961]).

Eleven Features of the Pioneer A.A. Group Program

I would now like to present below my own characterization of eleven specific features of the Pioneer A.A. Group Program; and, where I was able specifically to identify them, their biblical roots:

1. Abstinence--not one drop of alcohol was to be touched (inspired by Dr. William D. Silkworth as well as the revelation received by Henrietta Seiberling concerning Dr. Bob's drinking). See Dick B. *The Akron Genesis of Alcoholics Anonymous*, Newton ed. (Kihei, HI: Paradise Research Publications, 1997).

2. Medical help--in most cases, hospitalization (common in Akron and Cleveland).

3. Surrendering your life to God by accepting Jesus Christ as Lord and Saviour. (John 3:1-8, 16-17; 14:6; Acts 4:10-12; 16:30-31; Romans 10:9-10; Matt. 6:10.)

4. Finding and knowing God through Bible study, prayer, "revelation," reading, and church. (2 Timothy 2:15; Psalm 5:3; James 1:5, 2:10-11, 5:16; Isaiah 26:3; Matt. 6:25-33.)

5. Identifying and eliminating sin by inventorying one's sins, asking God's help in eliminating them, and obeying God's commandments. (Matthew 5:23-24, 7:3-5, 26:41; John 16:8; James 5:16, 4:7; Luke 6:31; 1 John 1:7-9; 4:20; Psalm 65:3; 51:4.)

6. Living love as exemplified in Jesus's Sermon on the Mount, 1 Corinthians 13, and the Book of James. (Matthew 5:43-45; 1 Corinthians 13:1-3, 13; James 2:8.)

7. Serving God and others as taught in the Bible and particularly by Jesus. (Mark 12:30-31; Mark 10:45; Romans 12:13; James 1:27, 2:15-16, 20.)

8. Fellowshipping with God through studying His Word, praying, asking guidance, and obeying God. (1 John 1:1-9; 3:2-9; 5:14-15; James 1:5-8, 21-25; 5:15-16; Psalm 5:3; 32:8; 37:5; 46:10; Proverbs 3:5-6; 1 Samuel 3:9; 2 Timothy 2:15; Acts 22:10.)

9. Fellowshipping with like-minded believers. (Matt.18:15-20; Acts 2:40-47; Romans 15:5-7; Philippians 2:1-5; 2 Thess. 3:6-9. And compare 2 Cor. 6:14–rejecting any activity that meant being "unequally yoked together with unbelievers.").

10. Witnessing without charge to what God has done and can do. (2 Corinthians 5:20; Acts 26:22-23, 5:29-32.)

11. Receiving power, healing, forgiveness, and deliverance. (Acts 1:8; Psalm 103:2-4; Romans 8:l, 12:1-2.)

2

A.A.'s Great Role
A Review of, and Experiences with, the
Practices, Principles, and Values of A.A.
in the 20th Century

A Personal Appraisal

Alcoholics Anonymous played an indispensable role in my own life over sixteen years ago. Without any reservation whatever as to the approach, it pointed me to the complete abandonment in my life of alcohol and mind-altering prescription drugs. Dependency on these potential poisons had brought me to ruin in every possible way. Moreover, A.A. prescribed for me a welcome discipline, when I had none, for avoiding booze and drugs. A.A. enabled me to end the almost unbearable loneliness that had descended upon me for many months, in the company of a gloomy depression. It gave me a purpose in, and technique for, helping others that I had never before grasped or used. It brought back to my mind and actions moral and religious values that had slipped into the gutter with progressive drinking and mind-destruction. And these were values I had seemingly ignored, yet long ago acquired, from my parents, from groups such as the Boy Scouts, from the American Legion's Boys State, from Sunday School and church, from my schools and colleges, from law school, and from such service organizations as the Chamber of Commerce and Rotary International. Surprisingly, A.A. even enabled me to replace a destroyed "normie"reputation with a modicum of self-esteem and significance in our kingdom of drunks! Most important of all, it spawned growing resurgence of my need for, and recognition of, God, the power of God, the commandments of God, the love of God, the forgiveness of God, my healing capabilities through God, and the

13

appreciation of His mercy and grace. As the Bible states twice in 1 John: God *is* love. And I needed Him in every area of my life. A.A. seemed to open the opportunity for me to seek Him and receive His help once again. Did I wind up freed of the drinking problem?" Yes–and from the day I walked in the doors of Alcoholics Anonymous.

After completing 11 years of research on the Biblical roots of early A.A. and publishing 17 titles on the subject, I have been deeply motivated to reiterate, primarily in the words of others, some of the major benefits that Alcoholics Anonymous has made available for me. Also made possible for others. And, despite all its warts and blisters, still offers to those willing to search (and without blinders) for all its real roots; to examine and analyze the actual specifics of those roots; and, where deserved, to acknowledge the unique, astonishing, and powerful offer to us all from A.A.'s 20th Century program practices.

Let's first look at some definition problems, and then at some of A.A.'s very significant and appropriately acknowledged values that were contributed in the last Century.

Some Valuable Ideas and Terminology

About God:

Early A.A. Relied upon the Creator. Early A. A. relied upon the Creator, Almighty God, *Yahweh*–using unmistakable, descriptive words about Him that were straight from the Bible. Our founders and their early friends all explicitly used such words and clearly did take them from the Bible. This unqualified and clear language referring to our Maker is unquestionably our most valuable legacy–whatever some of today's A.A. detractors may say or believe.

I have already thoroughly discussed and extensively documented **the Bible's and early A.A.'s references to the Creator**, Almighty God, whose name is Yahweh. (Dick B., *Why Early A.A. Succeeded: The Good Book in Alcoholics Anonymous Yesterday and Today*. [Kihei, HI: Paradise Research Publications, 2001], pp. 47-72; Dick B., *The Good Book and The Big Book: A.A.'s Roots in the Bible*, 2d ed. [Kihei, HI: Paradise Research Publications, 1998], pp. 49-88; Dick B., *Turning Point: A History of Early A.A.'s Roots and Successes* [Kihei, HI: Paradise Research Publications, 1997], pp. 252-53, 292-96; Dick B., *The Golden Text of A.A.: God, the Pioneers, and Real Spirituality* [Kihei, HI: Paradise Research Publications, 2000], pp. 5-39; and Dick B., *That Amazing Grace* [Kihei: HI: Paradise Research Publications, 1996], pp. 35-36, 50-52).

The First Edition of *Alcoholics Anonymous* Frequently Discusses God. In the First Edition of A.A.'s Big Book, our basic text, stated: "We never apologize to anyone for depending upon our Creator. . . . All men of faith have courage. They trust their God" (p. 81). Many other specific references to God as Creator can be found at pages 36, 39, 87, 93, 175, and elsewhere. The word "Creator" is used a total of 12 times in the basic text in each subsequent edition of the Big Book (*e.g. Alcoholics Anonymous*, 4th ed., pp. 13, 25, 28, 56, 68, 72, 75, 76, 80, 83, 158, 161). And the word "God" or specific references to Him can be found over 400 times in the Third Edition of the Big Book (Stewart C., *A Reference Guide to The Big Book of Alcoholics Anonymous* [Seattle, WA: Recovery Press, 1986], pp. 115-16).

Bill Wilson Discussed God. Bill Wilson himself often spoke of his "Father"in Biblical terms. Bill called Him God, Almighty God, Creator, Maker, Father, and Father of Lights, all titles easily located in the Good Book. Dr. Bob frequently spoke of Him as God and Heavenly Father, in terms that were–once again–taken from the Bible. A.A. Number Three (Bill Dotson) called Him God and Lord–once again using language from the Bible. Pioneer Clarence H. Snyder (who got sober in February of 1938, was sponsored by Dr. Bob, and later became the AA with the most sobriety) spoke often of God as Creator and Jesus Christ as God's Son. (See Dick B., *That Amazing*

Grace, pp. 35-36, 50-52.) I believe the impact of these specific descriptions and the beliefs they epitomized was so great that Bill put the following in italicized capital letters in the First Edition of his Big Book, *"WHO ARE YOU TO SAY THERE IS NO GOD?"* (p. 69). In the Big Book's Third Edition, there is an account by an early newcomer (whose name was Abby G.) and who returned from a ball game to see Wilson and Pioneer Clarence Snyder sitting on the davenport. Abby "challenged" Bill to tell him about A.A. and "to talk about 'this cure, this group of anonymous rummies'" (Mitchell K. *How It Worked: The Story of Clarence H. Snyder and The Early Days of Alcoholics Anonymous in Cleveland, Ohio.* [NY: A.A. Big Book Study Group, 1997], pp. 138-39). Abby "wanted to know what this was that worked so many wonders." In this man's own words: "and hanging over the mantel was a picture of Gethsemane and Bill pointed to it and said, 'There it is'" (*Alcoholics Anonymous*, 3rd ed., pp. 216-17). The "picture of Gethsemane," that was hanging on the wall, was, of course, a portrayal of Jesus–whose "transforming power and accomplishments" had in fact worked so many signs, miracles, *and* wonders–as reported in the Bible. See John 20:30; Mark 16:17-20; John 2:11; Acts 2:22: ("Ye men of Israel, hear these words: Jesus of Nazareth, a man approved of God among you by miracles and wonders and signs, which God did by him in the midst of you, as ye yourselves also know"); Acts 2:43: (". . . and many wonders and signs were done by the apostles"); Acts 4:29-30: "And now, Lord, behold their threatenings: and grant unto thy servants, that with all boldness they may speak thy word, By stretching forth thine hand to heal; and that signs and wonders may be done by the name of thy hold child Jesus"); Hebrews 2:3-4: ("How shall we escape, if we neglect so great salvation; which at the first began to be spoken by the Lord, and was confirmed unto us by them that heard *him*: God also bearing *them* witness, both with signs and wonders, and with divers miracles, and gifts of the Holy Ghost, according to his own will"); Romans 15:17-19: ("I have therefor whereof I may glory through Jesus Christ in those things which pertain to God. For I will not dare to speak of any of those things which Christ hath not wrought by me, to make the Gentiles obedient, by word and deed, Through mighty signs and wonders, by the power of the Spirit of God; so that from Jerusalem, and round about unto Illyricum, I have fully preached the gospel of Christ"). And there can be little doubt that Bill Wilson himself became fully conversant with such works of the Lord as Bill discussed them nightly with Dr. Bob in the summer of 1935 and listened daily to Dr. Bob's wife Anne read to Bill and Bob from the Gospels, Acts, Romans, and Hebrews. In fact, it was Anne herself who specifically recommended in her journal and teachings that one should read a book about the life of Christ each year, and study the Gospels, Acts, and the other church epistles daily. (Dick B., *Anne Smith's Journal, 1933-1939: A.A.'s Principles of Success.* 3rd ed. [Kihei, HI: Paradise Research Publications, 1998], pp. 81-88.)

The Grapevine **Spoke about God**. Another A.A. publication that spoke of cure by God and God alone was *The Grapevine* magazine. A.A.'s *Grapevine* later printed an article by the famous medical writer Paul de Kruif who wrote: "The AAs' medicine is God and God alone. This is their discovery." Realistically, de Kruif spoke of the medicine and the cure, stating, "It is free as air–with this provision: that the patients it cures have to nearly die before they can bring themselves to take it" (Dick B., *The Golden Text of A.A.*, pp. 69-70; see also *Volume II: Best of The Grapevine.* [New York: The AA Grapevine, Inc., 1986], pp. 202-03).

Morris Markey's Article in *Liberty Magazine* **Spoke about God**. Morris Markey had already written a much-quoted article in *Liberty Magazine* in 1939. The article was *Alcoholics and God.* The bold-face lead said: **"Is there hope for habitual drunkards? A cure that borders on the miraculous–and it works!"** (p. 6). Quoting Bill Wilson, the article stated: "I've got religion. . . . And **I know I'm cured of this drinking business** for good." [The article also reported that AAs will almost always say]: "I don't care what you call the Somebody Else. We call it God. . . . But the patient can have enough confidence in God–once he has gone through the mystical experience of recognizing God. And upon that principle the Alcoholic Foundation rests" (p. 6). As to this Morris Markey magazine article,

Bill Wilson said: "To our great delight, Morris soon hammered out an article which he titled 'Alcoholics and God'" (*Alcoholics Anonymous Comes of Age* [New York: Alcoholics Anonymous World Services, 1958], p. 177; see also Dick B., *The Golden Text of A.A.*, pp 70-71).

Harry Emerson Fosdick Wrote about God. Dr. Harry Emerson Fosdick frequently wrote about, and at A.A.'s own request, endorsed A.A.'s Big Book. Proudly quoting Fosdick's remarks, A.A. reported: "They agree that each man must have his own way of conceiving of God, but of God Himself they are utterly sure. . . ." (*Alcoholics Anonymous Comes of Age,* pp. 322-23; see also Dick B., *The Golden Text of A.A.*, pp. 69-71).

A.A.'s Four Religious Friends Who Championed God. Four friends of Alcoholics Anonymous who were non-alcoholics and from the field of religion had substantial input on the relationship with God that early AAs were enjoined to establish. There were A.A.'s later influential Roman Catholic friends who talked of God and God alone–Father Ed Dowling and Sister Ignatia. Their views as to Who was God were also echoed by A.A.'s spiritual well-spring–Rev. Sam Shoemaker, Rector of Calvary Episcopal Church in New York (whom Bill Wilson called a "co-founder of A.A.") and A.A.'s long-time friend and supporter Dr. Norman Vincent Peale.

  • **Father Ed Dowling**

    In November of 1940, Bill Wilson met the Irish Roman Catholic Jesuit priest Father Edward Patrick Dowling. Bill came to regard Father Ed as his "spiritual adviser." Still later, Bill asked Father Dowling to speak at A.A.'s St. Louis Convention in 1955. Dowling's biographer wrote: "Dowling's talk is remarkable in its explicit Roman Catholic Christianity offered in the steps of God to humanity." The biographer further quoted Dowling: "We know AA's Twelve Steps of man toward God" (Robert

Fitzgerald, S.J., *The Soul of Sponsorship: The Friendship of Fr. Ed Dowling, S.J. and Bill Wilson in Letters* [Center City, Minn: Hazelden, 1995], pp. 3, 13, 86-87). There can be no question that Fr. Dowling was speaking only of God as He is described in Scripture.

- **Sister Ignatia**

Bridget Della Mary Gavin had her roots in Ireland. Then, in America, she entered the convent of the Sisters of Charity of Saint Augustine, completed her postulancy, and petitioned the community for permission to wear their official habit, enter noviceship, and receive a new name, which became Sister Ignatia. She joined the A.A. scene about August 16, 1939–after A.A.'s Big Book had been published. Prior to her entry on the scene, Dr. Bob had hospitalized his newcomers in Akron's City Hospital. However, in about January, 1940, Sister Ignatia was able officially (with the knowledge of her superior and the Chief of Staff) to make hospital care available to AAs as patients of Dr. Bob's at St. Thomas Hospital in Akron, Ohio. She worked side-by-side with Dr. Bob for some 10 years thereafter. And she most assuredly talked to AAs about God Almighty during their brief hospitalization under her care. After completing their surrender–admitting defeat–her A.A. patients were often told that relinquishing alcohol's hold released the power of God into their lives. Only spiritual surrender, she said, involving admission of defeat, and acknowledgment of powerlessness, prompted the patients' search for God. She told them: The next step is to humbly turn to God. "Ask and you shall receive," she said. (See Jesus's Sermon on the Mount, Matt. 7:7-8: "Ask, and it shall be given you. . . . For every one that asketh receiveth."). In all her remarks, Sister Ignatia was speaking only of God as He is described in Scripture. (See Mary C. Darrah, *Sister Ignatia: Angel of*

Alcoholics Anonymous. [Chicago: Loyola University Press, 1992], pp. 14, 32-33, 42-43, 52-54, 87, 106-07).

- **Rev. Sam Shoemaker**

The Reverend Dr. Samuel Moor Shoemaker, Jr., was Rector of Calvary Episcopal Church in New York. From the very beginnings of A.A. in 1934 to the date of his death in 1963, Sam Shoemaker had the closest touch with Bill Wilson. Details can be found in Dick B., *New Light on Alcoholism: God, Sam Shoemaker, and A.A.*, 2d. ed. (Kihei, HI: Paradise Research Publications, 1999). Bill Wilson called Sam a "co-founder" of Alcoholics Anonymous. (See letter from Wilson to Shoemaker, dated April 23, 1963, quoted in Dick B. *New Light on Alcoholism*, 2d ed., p. 551). Shoemaker's colleagues called Sam a "Bible Christian" (Dick B., *The Oxford Group and Alcoholics Anonymous: A Design for Living That Works*, 2d ed. [Kihei, HI: Paradise Research Publications, 1998], p. 9). Bill Wilson had Sam address AAs at their International Conventions in both 1955 and 1960. (Dick B., *New Light on Alcoholism*, 2d ed., pp. 327-35.) And it is scarcely necessary to recount here the tremendous impact, in relationship, in language, and in presence, that Sam Shoemaker had on helping AAs to "find God"–God Almighty, the Creator, as He is described in Scripture.

- **Dr. Norman Vincent Peale**

The Reverend Dr. Norman Vincent Peale was a long-time friend of Bill Wilson's and a strong supporter of Alcoholics Anonymous. I had an interview with Dr. Peale for about one hour shortly before his death; and Peale stated to me he had never met anyone who did not think that the "higher power" of A.A. was God! Later, I was to read, in his best-selling book, many words to the same effect. It was God, as He is known and described in Scripture, that both Peale and

Wilson were talking about–even when referring to a "Higher Power" (Norman Vincent Peale. *The Positive Power of Jesus Christ: Life-Changing Adventures in Faith* [Pauling, NY: Foundation for Christian Living, 1980]; Norman Vincent Peale, *The Power of Positive Thinking* [Pauling, NY: Peale Center for Christian Living, 1978]).

Much has happened since the founding and developmental days of early A.A. when the Pioneers talked plainly about their establishment of a relationship with the Creator, their relying upon Him for deliverance, their learning about Him from the Bible, and their praying to Him on a daily basis. These biblical concepts are unquestionably a major part of the legacy bequeathed to us by early A.A. In plain-spoken words, therefore, the first and each subsequent edition of A.A.'s basic text have said (and with almost identical words each time):

Remember that we deal with alcohol–cunning, baffling, powerful! Without help it is too much for us. **But there is One who has all power–That One is God**. May you Find Him now! (*Alcoholics Anonymous*, 1st ed, p. 71; bold face added).

Our description of the alcoholic, the chapter to the agnostic, and our personal adventures before and after make clear three pertinent ideas: (a) That we were alcoholic and could not manage our own lives. (b) That **probably no human power could have relieved our alcoholism**. (c) That **God could and would if sought** (*Alcoholics Anonymous*, 1st ed., p. 72; bold face added).

I truly believed those propositions about God. A.A. had offered them to me right off the bat–and just about every single day after I had entered its rooms. I did seek relief from Almighty God, the Creator. And He has relieved my alcoholism for many many years and has done for me in many other areas of my life those things which I could not do for myself. That is A.A.'s great lesson to, and contribution for, me personally! At the time in my life I most needed them.

About Healing, Cure, Deliverance, and Overcoming

The concepts of healing, cure, deliverance, and overcoming predominated in pioneer A.A., and they provided a valuable awakening as to what God could do. But they soon took a back seat to the views of those who felt an alcoholic could never be "cured." The original concepts, however, are still a vital part of the A.A. legacy which offers to you, to me, and to all of us a very timely and special opportunity in this 21st Century.

A.A. Pioneer groups studied (and many believed) some very simple propositions about the help God can and does make available to those who want it. These propositions were stated over and over and over again in the Bible, from which the Pioneers obtained their basic ideas.

As to Healing. The first proposition is that God could and would and did heal them. The following are just a few of the Bible's assurances that early AAs read many many times. (For explicit documentation of the sources used by early AAs, including the Bible itself, from which AAs read about healing, cure, etc., see Dick B.: *The Golden Text of A.A.*, pp. 23-26.) Key Bible affirmation of their beliefs was and is found in these verses:

> . . . I am the Lord that healeth thee (Exodus 15:26b).

> Bless the Lord, O my soul. . . . Who forgiveth all thine iniquities; who healeth all thy diseases (Psalm 103:1, 3).

> Then they cry unto the Lord in their trouble, and he saveth them out of their distresses. He sent his word and healed them . . . (Psalm 107:19-20).

> . . . Thus saith the Lord, the God of David thy father. I have heard thy prayer. I have seen thy tears: Behold, I will heal thee . . . (2 Kings 20:5).

> I have seen his ways and will heal him (Isaiah 57:18).

For I will restore health unto thee, and I will heal thee of thy wounds, saith the Lord (Jeremiah 30:17).

See also: Matthew 11:5; Mark 10:52; Acts 3:16; James 5:15-16.

As to Curing Them. The second proposition is that God could and would cure them.

Behold, I will bring it health and cure, and I will cure them, and will reveal unto them the abundance of peace and truth (Jeremiah 33:6).

According to your faith be it unto you (Matthew 9:28).

The blind receive their sight, and the lame walk, the lepers are cleansed, and the deaf hear, the dead are raised up, and the poor have the gospel preached to them (Matthew 11:5).

And in that same hour he [Jesus] cured many of *their* infirmities and plagues, and of evil spirits; and unto many *that were* blind he gave sight (Luke 7:21).

Then he [Jesus] called his twelve disciples together, and gave them power and authority over all devils, and to cure diseases (Luke 9:1).

And he [Jesus] said unto them, Go ye and tell that fox [Herod], Behold, I cast out devils, and I do cures today and tomorrow, and the third *day* I shall be perfected (Luke 13:32).

Jesus saith unto him, Rise, take up thy bed, and walk. And immediately the man was made whole, and took up his bed, and walked: and on the same day was the sabbath. The Jews therefore said unto him that was cured, It is the sabbath day: it is not lawful for thee to carry *thy* bed (John 5:8-10. Interestingly, in A.A.'s Chapter "There Is A Solution," Bill states: "After such an approach many take up their beds and walk again." See *Alcoholics Anonymous*, 4th ed., p. 19).

See also Acts 5:15-16 (as to Peter), Acts 8:5-8 (as to Philip), Acts 10:38 (as to Jesus), and Acts 19:11-12 (as to Paul).

As to Deliverance: The third proposition is that they could claim deliverance.

> Who [the Father] hath delivered us from the power of darkness, and hath translated us into the kingdom of his dear Son (Colossians 1:13).

As to Overcoming: The fourth proposition is that those who were believers had overcome the world.

> Ye are of God, little children, and have overcome them: because greater is he that is in you, than he that is in the world (1 John 4:4).

> For whosoever is born of God overcometh the world: and this is the victory that overcometh the world, even our faith. Who is he that overcometh the world, but he that believeth that Jesus is the Son of God (1 John 5:4-5).

The foregoing propositions were *also* a part of my own cure, deliverance, and A.A. legacy. I firmly believed I would be healed of my alcoholism by sticking closely to the A.A. program, studying and learning the Big Book, taking and endeavoring to practice the relevant Steps, participating actively in the Fellowship, and passing on to others what I had received. On top of it all, I definitely relied upon the Creator for deliverance from the host of problems, including the liquor problem, all of which AAs rightly call the "wreckage" of the past. And God most assuredly did heal, cure, deliver, and enable me to overcome these destructive factors of my former life.

About "Alcoholism"

The puzzler concerns alcoholism itself: Was it, or is it a disease, a "sickness," a "spiritual malady," sin, a genetic disorder, a behavioral disorder, a mental disorder, or what? People are still working on that one, and A.A. eventually called it a three-part disease: mental, physical, and spiritual. Those A.A. ideas may well be outmoded today when it comes to the etiology of alcoholism. But the wisdom involved in A.A.'s description of the cure could serve us very well today if we would just accept it. A.A. described, and still describes, the cure as a "miracle." (See *Alcoholics Anonymous*, 4th ed., p. 85.) So did its Oxford Group predecessor, with its well-known slogan–"Sin is the disease. Christ–the Cure. The result–A Miracle" (Harry Almond. *Foundations For Faith* [London: Moral Re-Armament, 1975], pp. 1, 2, 7, 16; H. A. Walter, *Soul Surgery* [Oxford: University Press, 1932] p. 86). "It works–it really does," said the A.A. pioneers of their spiritual program of recovery from "alcoholism." And A.A. has repeated that statement in all its Big Book editions. (See *Alcoholics Anonymous*, 4th ed., p. 88.) A.A. worked! What's the legacy that can come from these simple expressions: "Disease," "Cure," "Jesus Christ," "Miracle?" Well, there might have been a legacy if the recovery world had "kept it simple," but it didn't. A.A. has therefore left a greater legacy in complicating the problem than it has in selling the solution.

The A.A. Haven for the Beleaguered Newcomer. Many a physician, clergyman, therapist, counselor, probation officer, judge, and educator says that nothing works as well as A.A. As I'll cover in more detail later, practically the first words I heard from my cardiologist here on Maui was that "A.A. is the only thing that works." I heard a similar idea from my psychiatrist when I first entered A.A. He said: "Get a Bible and a Big Book. Put a rubber band around them. And carry them wherever you go from now on." And–whatever the facts may be–Alcoholics Anonymous beckons when no one else knows what can be done for us or perhaps even wants to know.

Many of us, and I certainly was one, are a complete wreck when we walk in the doors of A.A. I was in a daze. I could not communicate very well. I had bitten my tongue almost in half from seizures. I was unable to think well or remember even the simplest things. I shook for months–even years thereafter. My legs and feet were numb. My left arm hurt so badly I could barely raise it at times. I wet my pants at A.A. meetings. I was severely depressed. And my legal, marital, criminal, financial, tax, and other problems seemed insoluble. I certainly did not know whether I had a disease, a spiritual malady, a sin, or a mental disorder. But I suffered from just about everything the devil could throw my way: fear, anxiety, guilt, shame, dishonesty, anger, remorse–all of these, and more. Serious or not, Bill Wilson expressed it well in his own Big Book story: "If there was a Devil, he seemed the Boss Universal, and he certainly had me" (Big Book, 1st ed., p. 20).

From my sponsor, from repetitive readings from A.A.'s Big Book, from endless jargon at meetings–some of it ridiculous and some of it helpful–and also from some good literature I picked up at my treatment center, I began to see and hear some important viewpoints about our plight:

> Many do not comprehend that the alcoholic is a very sick person (Foreword to First Edition of the *Alcoholics Anonymous*; quoted at page xiii of the new 4th edition).

> Remember that we deal with alcohol–cunning, baffling, powerful! Without help it is too much for us. But there is One who has all power–that One is God. May you find Him now! (4th ed., pp. 58-59).

> Probably no human power could have relieved our alcoholism. That God could and would if He were sought (4th ed., p. 60).

> RARELY HAVE we seen a person fail who has thoroughly followed our path (4th ed., p. 58).

> If you have decided you want what we have and are willing to go to any length to get it–then you are ready to take certain steps (4th ed., p. 58).

If we are painstaking about this phase of our development [moving through the Ninth Step], we will be amazed before we are half way through. . . . We will suddenly realize that God is doing for us what we could not do for ourselves (4th ed., pp. 83-84).

. . . For by this time [completion of the Tenth Step] sanity will have returned. We will seldom be interested in liquor. If tempted, we recoil from it as from a hot flame. We react sanely and normally, and we will see that this has happened automatically. We will see that our new attitude toward liquor has been given us without any thought or effort on our part. It just comes! That is the miracle of it (4th ed, p. 85).

You don't assimilate all those points at once. But you do hear them day after day at meeting after meeting. Soon they become part of your language and that of those with whom you talk. The ideas are not Gospel. You hear them while suffering from all kinds of trouble and physical sickness. In my case, though I did not once or ever want to take a drink, I still wondered how you could possibly get through all the trouble. Ever!

And that's when God can and should become the most important single factor in your life. They'll tell you in A.A. that staying sober is the most important thing. Maybe it is. However, being healed of the drinking problem is a small victory compared to being cured of all the rest of the consequences–heart, liver, balance, breathing, insomnia, and other physical damage. Overcoming drinking pales in comparison to being delivered from the fears, doubts, worries, shame, guilt, anxiety, confusion, forgetfulness, depression, and endless legal troubles. Without help, it's too much for us. And that's when God becomes the most important single factor in your life. At least in my life. Or did I already say that!

Back to the Problem–Alcoholism: What Is It? There is no reliable legacy for us from A.A. which satisfactorily answers the question: "What is alcoholism?" Is alcoholism a disease, a spiritual malady, a sin, a sickness, a genetic disorder, a physical addiction, a psychological addiction, a mental disorder, an hereditary burden, an environmental product, or what? And can it be healed or cured or cast out or overcome or reversed, or treated, or what? Or, in today's A.A. language, are we still in bondage, because: "What we really have is a daily reprieve contingent on the maintenance of our spiritual condition" (*Alcoholics Anonymous*, 4th ed., p. 85)? And hence, says A.A.'s text: "We are not cured of alcoholism" (*Alcoholics Anonymous*, 4th ed., p. 85) These are heavy issues, I am sure. Their discussion envelopes tens of thousands of articles. But the issues really don't matter much to me today or to most of us who think our solution lies with God. They probably matter a great deal to those who spend money on insurance, treatment, grants, research, prevention, correction, TV ads, education, and religious programs. Seemingly looking for some "magic" bullet or formula. But the experts are in total disagreement anyway. Unfortunately, however, that's where the money seems to be going–just throwing money at alcoholism through insurance, grants, agencies, research, therapy, government wars, Czars, and on and on.

- **E. M. Jellinek**

    Since A.A. is regarded as favoring the "disease concept of alcoholism," a good starting place in trying to describe alcoholism is *The Disease Concept of Alcoholism* by E. M. Jellinek (New Jersey, Hillhouse Press, 1960). To begin with, Jellinek jests: "there are more definitions of definition than there are 'definitions' of alcoholism" (p. 33). And his own learned study raises more questions than it answers. Dealing with alcoholism and its species, Jellinek discusses *alpha*, *beta*, *gamma*, and *delta* alcoholism, stating that *gamma* alcoholism involves a definite progression from psychological to physical dependence and marked behavior changes with acquired increased tissue tolerance to alcohol, adaptive cell metabolism, withdrawal symptoms and "craving," and loss of control. Whew! This *gamma* species, he says, produces the greatest and most serious kinds of damage (pp. 35-41). Discussing various formulations, he covers alcoholism in physiopathological and physical terms, including these: allergy, brain pathology, nutrition, and endocrinology. Jellinek puts A.A.'s view under the "allergy" category. In summary, Jellinek can be listed with those who, for one reason or another, and despite all the variations and complexities, regard alcoholism as a "disease."

But the battle merely begins at that point, and we will mention several of those whose somewhat different and even later views seem to command a good deal of respect in various circles.

- **George Vaillant, M.D..**

  The distinguished scientist and professor George E. Vaillant–who has recently won for himself a spot in the A.A. hierarchy itself–observes in *The Natural History of Alcoholism Revisited*. (Mass: Harvard University Press, 1995): "Alcoholism is a disorder of great destructive power. . . . Perhaps the best one-sentence definition of alcoholism available to us is the one provided by the National Council on Alcoholism (1976, p. 764): 'The person with alcoholism cannot consistently predict on any drinking occasion the duration of the episode or the quantity that will be consumed.' As with coronary heart disease, we must learn to regard alcoholism as both disease and behavior disorder" (pp. 1, 45).

- **Herbert Fingarette**

  Herbert Fingarette, a much respected professor at the University of California, a consultant on alcoholism and addiction to the World Health Organization, and a Fellow of the Stanford Center for Advanced Studies in the Behavioral Sciences, has posted a new mark to shoot at. The title of his book speaks eloquently of his position: *Heavy Drinking: The Myth of Alcoholism as a Disease*. (Berkeley and Los Angeles: University of California Press, 1988). Showing no disinclination to enter controversy, Fingarette writes: "Once we free ourselves of the discredited classic disease concept, we no longer limit our attention to a relatively small group of diagnosed alcoholics whose drinking behavior allegedly derives from a single causal origin and follows a single inexorable course. Instead we perceive a much larger and more diverse assortment of individual heavy drinkers who have little in common except that (1) they drink a lot, (2) they tend to have many more problems in life than nondrinkers or moderate drinkers, and (3) they show a puzzlingly inconsistent ability to manage their drinking" (p. 99). As to alcoholics, he says: "The broad interpretation that best fits the evidence is that heavy drinkers are people for whom drinking has become a central activity in their way of life. . . for the long-term heavy drinker, life has come to center on drinking–life [that] is pervaded by a preoccupation with drinking, shaped and driven by the quest for drink, drinking situations, and drinking friends" (p. 100). The professor makes the following additional points: (1) There is no single entity which can be defined as alcoholism. (2) There is no clear dichotomy between either alcoholics and non-alcoholics, or between prealcoholics and nonprealcoholics even though individuals may have differing susceptibility to both the use of alcohol and the development of alcohol problems as a result of genetic, physiological, psychological, and sociocultural factors. (3) The sequence in which adverse consequences develop appears to be highly variable. (4) There is no evidence to date for a basic biological process that predisposes an individual toward abuse of alcohol. (5) The **empirical evidence suggests that alcohol problems are reversible**. (6) Alcohol problems are typically interrelated with other life problems" (p. 106). Finally, he adds: "There is no reason to see heavy drinking as a symptom of illness, a sign of persistent evil, or the mark of a conscienceless will" (p. 111).

• **Lance Dodes, M.D.**

Lance Dodes is a psychiatrist and psychoanalyst, Assistant Clinical Professor of Psychiatry at Harvard Medical School, and a Director of the Boston Center for Problem Gambling. He has served as the director of alcoholism and substance abuse treatment unit at Harvard's McLean Hospital, and as the director of the alcoholism unit at what is now a part of Massachusetts General Hospital. He has just published a very challenging work, titled *The Heart of Addiction* (New York: HarperCollins Publishers, 2002). Dodes rejects the disease concept of alcoholism and the idea that it is a genetic disorder. He says treatment ideas have become stuck. Of A.A., he says: "Considering Alcoholics Anonymous, for instance, two studies cited by Fingarette that looked at eighteen-month followups of people in AA found that at most, 25 percent of people were still attending meetings, and that among regular AA members, only 22 percent consistently maintained sobriety. Taken together, these numbers indicate that fewer than 6 percent of people both attended and stayed sober" (p. 9). Dodes advocates a new way of understanding alcoholism and states "of people with alcoholism and other addictions who have been able to take control of their lives by making use of the new way to understand the nature of addiction. . . [and] understood for themselves how the critical kinds of emotional factors worked in *them*, they were just like anyone else who has discovered the basis for what he or she is doing. **Armed with this deeper understanding of their compulsion to repeat their addictive behavior, *they were no longer helpless in the face of it*** " (p. 9; bold face added). He claims addictions are always displacements–substitutions for another, more direct act; and, that without displacement, responding to overwhelming helplessness would mean taking a direct action. Further, "without a displacement, there can be no addiction. The fact that addictions are displacements also explains why people can shift so easily from one addiction to another. They are simply moving the *focus of their displacement* to a new activity" (pp. 54-55). He continues: ". . . despite their particular form, all addictions are related. . . . The underlying unity of addictions also leads to a new perspective on their names–they are simply the names of displaced focuses. 'Alcoholism,' for example, is the title when the purpose and drive of an addiction is displaced to the behavior of drinking alcohol" (p. 56). "*Addictions,*" he says, "*are inherently psychological compromises.* The very fact of performing an addictive act means that, for reasons that are emotionally important to you, you did not allow yourself to take direct action. . . . Unlike the common wisdom that addictions are a form of pleasure-seeking, the fact that they are self-imposed compromises indicates how much they are the opposite. Rather than being the simple enactment of an impulse toward pleasure, addictions are a sign of *inhibiting* an action that would have directly expressed your wish at that moment" (p. 57). Drawing a firm distinction between physical addiction and psychological addition, Dodes states: "Detoxifying (withdrawing) people who are physically addicted to their drugs does not cure them. Not only do people often relapse immediately after detoxification, but it is well-known that addictive behavior frequently returns even many years after the last drug use. Clearly, the essence of the addiction exists separately and independently from the presence of physical effects brought about by the drug itself, or by withdrawal from the drug" (p. 72). "Addiction is a human problem that resides in people, not in the drug or in the drug's capacity to produce physical effects. . . . Some people, while agreeing that the problem of addiction lies in the person and not in the drug or its physical effects, would attribute the problem to genes, or to brain chemistry, rather than to a person's psychology. . . . An addiction, then, is truly present only when there is a psychological drive to perform the addictive behavior–that is, only when there is psychological addiction. For this reason, I call behaviors in which this psychology is present *true addictions*, in contrast to cases in which there is only a physical addiction" (pp. 73-74). "If unquestionable addictions can be present without any physical addiction–as with binge drinkers or compulsive gamblers–and if physical addictions can be present without any true addiction–as in the medically ill patients I just mentioned–then it must be that physical addiction is neither necessary to nor sufficient for an addiction. It can truthfully be said, then, that physical addiction is surprisingly incidental to the real nature of addiction" (pp. 75-76). Dr. Dodes gives a light nod of approval to A.A. as being useful for some people while noting its ineffectiveness for most. However, he also gives a light nod of recognition to "higher power" ideas. Yet, adopting his profession's all too frequent attitude about religion, he makes no mention whatever of God, the Bible, the power of Jesus Christ, or the Christian Fellowship and distinct biblical focus of the early A.A. program.

- **Joan Matthews Larson, Ph.D.**

Joan Mathews Larson holds a doctorate in nutrition and is founder of Health Recovery Center in Minneapolis. In consultation with Keith W. Sehnert, M.D., she wrote *Alcoholism–The Biochemical Connection: A Biomedical Regimen for Recovery with a Proven 75 Percent Success Rate* (New York: Villard Books, 1992). She said: "The more I learned about alcoholism, the more I became convinced that it is not just a psychological disorder or a sign of emotional weakness or flawed character that can be resolved with talk therapy. Instead, I began to see alcoholism as a physical disease, the outcome of a powerful physical addiction to alcohol that gradually inflicts mortal damage to brain and body chemistry" (p. 23). She advocates that alcoholism has many biochemical connections and is not primarily a psychological disorder. Citing dismal recovery rates among those with no treatment, with antabuse only, and even with full treatment including A.A., she asserts that relapse is the norm. She observed that the majority of her patients suffered from one or more of five disorders: 1. Nutritional deficits. 2. Food allergies. 3. Thyroid disorders. 4. Hypoglycemia. 5, Candida-related complex. Her biochemical repair program addresses substances like alcohol and other drugs that must be kept out of the alcoholic's body and substances that must be restored (brain and body chemicals depleted by alcohol). For example, her detox and maintenance formulae involve glutamine, free-form amino acids, DL-Phenylalanine, Triptophan, Vitamin C, Calcium/Magnesium, Efamol. Multivitamin/mineral formula, and pancreatic enzymes. Attention is paid to other factors such as diet, exercise, and so on.

- ### Gerald G. May M.D.

Gerald G. May deals with alcoholism and addictions from his stance as a Christian psychiatrist. His important title is *Addiction & Grace: Love and Spirituality in the Healing of Addictions.* (San Francisco: Harper and Collins, 1988). In brief, Dr. May says that our free will is given to us for a purpose: so that we may choose freely, without coercion or manipulation, to love God in return for His love, and to love one another in a similar perfect way. Our freedom, he says, is not complete. Working against it is the powerful force of addiction. Psychologically, he says, addiction uses up desire. It is like a psychic malignancy, sucking our life energy into specific obsessions and compulsions, leaving less and less energy available for other people and other pursuits. Spiritually, he contends, addiction is a deep-seated form of idolatry. The objects of our addictions become our false gods. These are what we worship, attend to, and to which we give our time and energy, instead of love. "Addiction, then, displaces and supplants God's love as the source and object of our deepest true desire. It is . . . a 'counterfeit of religious presence'." (p. 13). Dr. May gives this as the definition of addiction: "Addiction is any compulsive, habitual behavior that limits freedom of human desire. It is caused by the attachment of desire to specific objects. . . . [and he adds] As we shall see, the relationship between attachment and addiction is not as simple as it might sound. For one thing, the brain never completely forgets its old attachments, so the absence of conscious desire does not necessarily mean attachment is gone. . . it is obvious that still more precision is needed to adequately understand the nature of addiction. We can take a significant step toward precision [May claims] by exploring five essential characteristics that mark true addiction: (1) tolerance; (2) withdrawal symptoms, (3) self-deception, (4) loss of willpower, and (5) distortion of attention" (pp. 24-26).

- **William L. Playfair, M.D.**

In *The Useful Lie* (Illinois: Crossway Books, 1991), William L. Playfair, a Christian physician, attacks the "Recovery Industry" and the "Disease Model" of alcoholism and with a much different approach. First, Playfair points to authors like Professor Fingarette who consider unscientific and counterproductive the idea that alcoholism and drug addiction are "diseases" requiring medical treatment. Second, Playfair believes that the "disease" concept has been swallowed by Christians and rendered churches as ineffective as the treatment industry. Third, he states: "Not too long ago Christians and non-Christians alike believed that what is today referred to as 'alcoholism' or 'drug addition'–'chemical dependency'–was the consequence of the regular and long-term 'sinful' use of alcohol and drugs. In the case of alcohol, it simply meant excessive drinking. . . . According to this traditional view, most drug users became addicts by misusing or abusing drugs. It is that simple. The earlier traditional view is called the *moral model*. The recovery industry's view is called the *medical model*. While the moral model recognizes that medical problems often result from or are complicated by substance abuse, it sees addiction as primarily a moral problem with a moral solution." Stating that he uses the term moral model to refer to the Biblical view, he paints this picture of the Moral Model: (1) The addict became addicted primarily as the result of *immoral behavior*. (2) The addict is first and foremost *guilty of sin*. (3) The addict is *spiritually* and *morally depraved*. On page 29 and 30, Dr. Playfair musters compelling Scripture to establish that those addicted to alcohol are called drunkards; that the alcoholic or drug addict is a person *controlle*d by his or her habit; that the Christian is to be "controlled" by the Holy Spirit; that we have a choice in such matters; that substance abuse or misabuse has brought these people "under the power," and that such "uncontrolled lifestyle" is called unrighteousness (sin). Playfair finds company for his views in the work of a number of authors such as Dr. Martin Bobgan and his wife Deidre Bobgan.

• **Martin and Deidre Bobgan**

Martin and Deidre Bobgan, a husband and wife team, authored *12 Steps to Destruction: Codependency Recovery Heresies* (Santa Barbara, CA: EastGate Publishers, 1991). The Bobgans quote the following: "When man defines disease, alcoholism becomes a disease. Then all manner of sin is labeled as disease, to be cured with chemical, electrical and mechanical treatments. Any sinful habit, from gluttony to fornication, from stealing to bestiality, can become a disease" (p. 86). Firing shots at A.A., the Bobgans say: "The influence of AA has been tremendous in promoting the belief that habitual heavy drinking is a "disease" of alcoholism. In spite of the fact that there is no clear etiology for the disease, most people now assume alcoholism is indeed a disease. And, even though the Bible clearly refers to drunkenness as sin, most Christians have hopped onto the AA bandwagon of faith and believe that habitual drunkenness is due to a disease called 'alcoholism' or 'addiction' rather than to sin" (p. 74).

- **Jerry G. Dunn**

Jerry G. Dunn is an ordained Baptist pastor. But, much before his ordination, and after completing college, he had sought a promising career in the field of advertising. Then, he "was gripped in alcohol's unyielding vise." He lost everything. The road down led to a Texas prison where, through reading the Bible, he was saved. Later he enjoyed a successful career in the newspaper business, did extensive counseling of alcoholics, and finally joined the staff of the Open Door Mission in Omaha where he became Director of Rehabilitation. I personally met him years later. By that time, he had written the very popular title *God Is for the Alcoholic*. (Chicago, Moody Press, 1965). We shared a podium together at the first International Conference of Alcoholics Victorious. He gave me a copy of his book. And I found he laid his views of alcoholism right on the line and very concisely. "Alcohol," he said, "is a poison to the nervous system. . . . Beverage alcohol is an intoxicating, hypnotic analgesic, an anesthetic narcotic, poisonous and potentially habit-forming, craving-producing or addiction-producing drug or chemical. . . . alcohol itself plays more of a role in the process of alcoholism than just that of causing intoxication" (p. 13). "Alcoholism is a sickness of the soul–a sin sickness, and it must be considered such," said Jerry (p. 21). He cited some 627 verses in the Bible on excessive drinking. He said: "There isn't any place in the Bible where it says that you shouldn't drink. But it does have a lot to say about getting drunk," he tells a listener. "Then I proceed to show him in the Word that he is a sinner, that he needs a Saviour because he has committed a sin against the Holy God by getting drunk" (p. 71).

- **Jack Van Impe**

In *Alcohol: The Beloved Enemy*–written by Jack Van Impe, with Roger F. Campbell (Nashville: Thomas Nelson Publishers, 1980)–Dr. Van Impe lends much support to Jerry Dunn's position. Van Impe does a concise and forceful job of setting forth what he believes to be the Bible's position on drink, drunkenness, and "alcoholism." He provides lots of data on the destructiveness of drinking and on "the rising tide of alcohol use in America." He also covers the ineffective results in the Washingtonians, the Temperance Movement, the Anti-Saloon League, Prohibition, etc. But his major platform rests on his answers to these questions: "Do Christians always agree on the booze question? Should they? What does the Bible say about beverage alcohol?" (p. 100). He says that Christians are divided on the question of drinking. In America, he states, the majority of evangelical churches take at least a nominal stand against the use of alcohol; but the move is on to water down this position. In Europe, a great number of professing Christians use wine or beer regularly under the guise of necessity, he claims. Then he asks: Is there no biblical absolute on the alcohol question? First, he tackles "wine in the Old Testament." He points to authoritative biblical studies he says establish that the Bible speaks of two kinds of wine: good wine and bad wine, unfermented wine and fermented wine, wine that does not intoxicate and wine that does intoxicate. He concludes that wherever the use of wine is prohibited or discouraged it [the Bible] means the fermented wine. Where its use is encouraged and is spoken of as something for our good it means unfermented" (p.118). Then Van Impe covers "Jesus and Wine." This means wine at the Communion service and the wine given to Jesus on the Cross. In the one case, he says, Jesus remained consistent as to fermented wine "when establishing the Communion service and therefore did not use intoxicating wine as the symbol of His blood" (p. 128). On the cross, he says, Jesus was offered intoxicating wine to make the pain more bearable. Van Impe says: "In His most trying hour, Jesus refused intoxicating wine. And so should we" (p. 129). He then reviews "wine in the church." Citing a biblical scholar, he says: "In the light of the conclusions drawn earlier that there is no explicit Old Testament justification for assuming that wine drinking is ever appropriate for the saint, even in moderation, it is important to indicate briefly that the New Testament evidence concurs with, or at least is not contrary to, this conclusion" (p. 137). Then, he concludes that, even in the case of wine for the sick, whether it was fermented or unfermented: "In either case, the text provides no encouragement for the use of fermented wine except for the sick. . . . In the finest hour of the church, beverage alcohol was shunned by earnest and dedicated believers" (p. 139). Van Impe argues that "everyone who drinks has an alcohol problem"–whether drink simply dulls the senses of the user, or carries with it the threat of dependency, or makes one periodically hazardous to others." Or causes physical maladies, family problems, behavior changes, law breaking, and so on. And on our basic question, Van Impe concludes: "My belief is that alcoholism is one of the symptoms of a far deeper and more serious disease. . . . **The underlying disease is sin**. These [things such as bad temper, cruelty, greed, hypocrisy, compulsive promiscuity, fear, etc.] are the outbreaking manifestations of it. As spots go with measles, boils with blood impurities, and certain rashes with emotional stress, these things go with sin. If this is true, we can only have a real cure **when the basic disease has been cured. . . . I believe that all those people I mentioned who don't need to drink anymore have been cured of their real underlying disease, which was sin. Inevitably, the symptom–alcoholism–went away**" (pp. 154-55; bold face added).

- **Cathy Burns**

In *Alcoholics Anonymous Unmasked: Deception and Deliverance* (Mt. Carmel, PA: Sharing, 1991), Dr. Cathy Burns sets forth a similar view. She says: "Actually, if alcoholism is a disease, it is the easiest 'disease' to cure. All one has to do is stay away from alcoholic beverages. . . . Diseases such as cancer, measles, mumps, and tuberculosis certainly are not controlled in any such way" (p. 69). She continues: "No, alcoholism is NOT a disease; it is a sin which is willfully committed by a person" (p. 70). She includes an entire chapter, titled "The Bible And Alcoholism" (pp. 93-105); and she concludes: "The answer to overcoming an alcoholic lifestyle (or any other sin) is not found in attending Alcoholics Anonymous meetings, but confessing your sins to Jesus and asking Him to forgive you" (pp. 103-104). She cites Romans 10:9; Psalm 32:5; Romans 5:1; Philippians 4:7; and Matthew 11:28; and then reminds: "If the Son [Jesus Christ] therefore shall make you free, ye shall be free indeed" (John 8:36).

There are many other writers who have taken a crack at definitions–often with an apparent attempt to attack religion, Christianity, Alcoholics Anonymous, the "recovery industry," addiction medicine, treatment programs, certain scholars, certain historians, and many other kinds of targets. But most will not receive our attention here. And their writings can be found listed and/or categorized in our inventory of the 23,100 item historical collection I have assembled over the last 11 years and in connection with my 17 published titles. That material is now embodied in my title *Making Known the Biblical History and Roots of Alcoholics Anonymous: An Eleven-Year Research, Writing, Publishing, and Fact Dissemination Project* (Kihei, HI: Paradise Research Publications, 2001).

Other Definitions and Viewpoints. Helpful, perhaps, are the following titles containing definitions and viewpoints on the meaning of alcoholism and addiction:

• **Ronald J. Catanzaro, M.D.**

For the purpose of this book, an alcoholic is defined as a person who has become dependent on the drug alcohol, consequently drinking more alcohol than the socially accepted norm for his culture; his excessive drinking damages his health and his relation to his family, friends and job. Alcoholism is the name of the chronic disease from which the alcoholic suffers (*Alcoholism: The Total Treatment Approach* [IL: Charles C. Thomas Publisher, 1968], p. 6).

• **Arnold M. Washton, Ph.D. & Donna Boundy, M.S.W.**

. . . [A]ddiction is any self-defeating behavior that a person cannot stop despite its adverse consequences. . . . (*Willpower's Not Enough: Understanding and Recovering from Addictions of Every Kind* [NY: Harper & Row, 1989], p. 13).

• **James E. Royce, S.J.**

Alcoholism was portrayed there [in the previous chapter] as a complex, psychophysiological dependence upon alcohol which ends up being its own obsessive-compulsive dynamism (*Alcohol Problems and Alcoholism: A Comprehensive Survey* [NY: The Free Press, 1981], p. 159).

- **Edward P. Nace, M.D.**

Six constructs make up the essential phenomena of alcoholism: Psychological dependence on a chemical, craving, loss of control, personality regression, denial, and conflicted behavior" (*The Treatment of Alcoholism* [NY: Brunner/Mazel, Publishers, 1987], p. 67).

- **Katherine Ketcham, et al.**

Alcoholism is a progressive neurological disease strongly influenced by genetic vulnerability. Inherited or acquired abnormalities in brain chemistry create an altered response to alcohol which in turn causes a wide array of physical, psychological, and behavioral problems. . . . Alcoholism is caused by biochemical/neurophysiological abnormalities that are passed down from one generation to the next or, in some cases, acquired through heavy or prolonged drinking (Ketcham, et al., *Beyond the Influence: Understanding and Defeating Alcoholism* [New York: Bantam Books, 2000], p. 46).

- **Anderson Spickard M.D. and Barbara R. Thompson**

Because of the alcoholic's helplessness, and because addiction follows a predictable pattern and has a pronounced inheritance factor, it is not inappropriate to call alcoholism a disease. However, it is never simply a physical disease; rather, alcoholism is the paradigm disease of the whole person. . . the alcoholic, more often than not, loses everything. He is sick in his body, mind, emotions, spirit, and relationships. Unless the alcoholic gets help in all four areas, his chances for recovery are very poor indeed (*Dying for a Drink: What You Should Know about Alcoholism* [Waco, TX: Word Books, 1985], p. 41).

• **Wayne Poley, Gary Lea, and Gail Vibe**

From the old moralistic perspective, "weakness of will" would probably be held up as a major cause of alcoholism, while a biological-medical model would look for nutritional deficits or metabolic disorders and a psychologist might try to uncover a "personality disorder." Much closer to providing us with an accurate perspective of how alcoholism develops would be the contemporary multi-disciplinary model: alcoholism is the resultant end-product of a variety of contributing factors, from socio-cultural to biological to psychological (*Alcoholism: a Treatment Manual* [NY: Gardner Press, 1979], p. 33).

• **Martin M. Davis**

Addiction–whether chemical, behavioral, or relational–is first and foremost a spiritual disease. It is an attempt to escape the 'pain, brokenness, and human limitation' of our existence in this fallen world. Pain, brokenness, and human limitation are spiritual problems that emanate from the atrophy of the soul that characterizes human beings who have been cut off from the life-giving sustenance of the Creator. Chemical dependency and other forms of addiction frequently result from maladaptive attempts to find the solace that comes only from a spiritual relationship with the God who is there. Addiction is often the unfortunate result of innumerable misguided attempts to fill the emptiness of our thirsty souls with chemicals or inappropriate behaviors. Addiction is a spiritual disease because it offers a counterfeit substitute for the soul-healing that can come only from a personal relationship with Jesus Christ (*The Gospel and the Twelve Steps: Developing a Closer Relationship with Jesus* [San Diego, CA: Recovery Publications, 1993], p. 202-03).

• **Bob and Pauline Bartosch**

Although a portion of the Christian community considers alcoholism and drug dependency to be a "sin" or merely a spiritual problem, *we believe addiction to be a disease of body, mind, emotion and soul,* and that all aspects of the person need to be addressed in order for quality recovery to occur *(Overcomers Outreach: A Bridge to Recovery* [La Habra, CA: Overcomers Outreach, 1994], p. 55).

• **J. Keith Miller**

The idea of referring to Sin as a "disease" troubles some people, who think I am saying that one is not responsible for one's sinful behavior. In other words, if Sin is a disease and I can't help myself, why not go on and sin. I'm not saying that at all, but merely stating what biblical theologians have always known: Sin is a pernicious condition that all have (1 John 1:9) and that we can't defeat on our own. Otherwise why would Christ have to "come and save us from sin"? Sin is like compulsive or addictive habits that seem to control our actions even when we don't want them to and after we swear we will "never do it again." Paradoxically, even though we are powerless to defeat Sin on our own, we are responsible for our Sin and for seeking to stop sinning, a seeking that leads us to God. . . . But I finally realized that nobody could help me with my Sin, my control disease, and the fear and pain it was causing me. The source of this pain was inside myself in my invisible and "benevolent," but self-centered and myopic, "conductor of the local world attitude." . . . Only God's power can defeat our Sin, but part of what God's power does is release the personal power he has given each of us as creatures in his image. As we begin to access God's power to defeat the Sin-disease and discover and use our own legitimate power to live, we step into the spiritual world, where God shares the keys to life and reality *(A Hunger for Healing: The Twelve Steps As a Classic Model for Christian Spiritual Growth* [NY: HarperCollins, 1991], pp. 4-6).

- **David R. Rudy**

  An Interactionist Definition. . . . Alcoholism is a characterization attached to drinkers by others when these others question the drinkers' behavior and when the drinkers lack the power or desire to negotiate another explanation. . . . Before we examine this definition in detail, the reader must be aware that it is not the same to say that alcoholism is a characterization that involves behavior and response as it is to say that alcoholism is sin, moral weakness, crime, or illness. The latter definitions are definitions of phenomena as social problems while the former is a sociological definition (*Becoming Alcoholic: Alcoholics Anonymous and the Reality of Alcoholism* [IL: Southern Illinois University Press, 1986], pp. 99-100).

Two Additional, Voluminous Research Works. While not necessarily taking a particular position, these two do illustrate and, in the first case, compound the array of complex and confusing discussions of drunkenness, sin, and the uncontrolled use of alcohol and drugs.

- **William L. White. *Slaying The Dragon: The History of Addiction Treatment and Recovery in America*** (Bloomington, IL: Chestnut Health Systems, 1998). The title contains an immense amount of valuable information, some of which will be quoted here. The problem is that it purports to be a comprehensive history. Yet, like so much of the other historical writing of the last twenty-five years, it completely misses the boat when it comes to describing, analyzing, or covering spiritual roots of Alcoholics Anonymous–the movement it most applauds. Those roots, primarily biblical, are covered comprehensively and in depth in many of my titles, including *Turning Point: A History of Early A.A.'s Spiritual Roots and Successes* (Kihei, HI: Paradise Research Publications, 1997), and http://www.dickb.com/index.shtml. White's work exemplifies just one more glaring omission by today's secular writers in their failure to provide accurate data on the Bible, Quiet Time, the teachings of Rev. Samuel M. Shoemaker, the life-changing program of the Oxford Group, the journal of Anne Ripley Smith (wife of A.A. co-founder Dr. Bob), and the Christian literature in such wide use by the A.A. pioneers. In other words, a purported history that omits major, early historical elements of its subject matter, can only be called a *review* of *some* history, *but not a history*. Nonetheless, White's material contains these important and helpful points: "The Swedish physician Magnus Huss introduced the term *alcoholism* in 1849 to describe a state of chronic alcohol intoxication that was characterized by severe physical pathology and disruption of social functioning" (p. xiv). White closes his chapter on the A.A. program by stating: "A.A.'s legacies are many. First, A.A. constitutes the largest and most enduring mutual aid-society of recovered alcoholics in human history. . . . A.A. also constitutes the most fully developed culture of recovery that has ever existed–a culture with its own history, mythology, values, language, rituals, symbols, and literature. . . . A.A. has also exerted an enormous influence on the evolution of social policies related to alcohol and alcoholism, and on the evolution of alcoholism treatment. . . . A.A. survived the demise of its founders as a 'stunning innovation in the politics of organizational life' and a unique 'democratic solution to the succession problem inherent in charismatic leadership. . . . A.A. was the modern beginning of social affiliation based on shared experience. A.A. marks the apex of new voluntary spiritual communities that have increasingly taken over the functions of family, extended family, and neighborhood, as well as the social functions of the church and workplace" (pp. 162-163). Wow and Amen! I didn't realize how important my fellowship of drunks actually is. **Yet in response to all the foregoing A.A. accolades, I comment in amazement: You didn't mention**

God! How, then, can this be called an adequate history of A.A! The situation reminds me of one described by a man who is probably the most popular A.A. circuit speaker of today. He tells of a sign in Germany which states, *"God is dead," signed "Nietzsche"* [referring to the German philosopher Friedrich Wilhelm Nietzsche].The sentence on the sign, says the A.A. speaker, is followed by this statement: *"Nietzsche is dead," signed "God."* Is God dead in the alcoholism field? Impossible, but some of its most popular writers talk as if He were. But He isn't!

• **Howard Clinebell.** *Understanding and Counseling Persons with Alcohol, Drug, and Behavioral Addictions* (Nashvillle, Abingdon Press, 1998–rev. and enlarged ed.) is one of more than a dozen books by this distinguished Professor Emeritus, School of Theology at Claremont, California. Clinebell has been on the alcoholism scene since the earliest days of A.A. His work is a compendium of information and instruction for "Counseling for Recovery and Prevention Using Psychology and Religion." Clinebell begins this particular work with definitions of addiction and alcoholism: "In traditional psychiatric usage, the term *addiction* is limited to obsessive-compulsive abuse of substances like alcohol and drugs. . . . The compulsive-addictive uses of alcohol are recognized as an illness by both the World Health Organization of the United Nations and the American Medical Association. . . . *Alcohol addiction* is roughly synonymous with *alcoholism.* . . . *Chronic alcoholism* usually refers to the advanced stages of the illness. It is during these stages that physiological and psychiatric complications most frequently occur. These complications are the physical and psychological diseases resulting from the prolonged, excessive use of alcohol and include polyneuropathy, pellagra, cirrhosis of the liver, Korsakoff's psychosis, delerium tremens, acute alcoholic hallucinosis, and others" (pp. 24-25). Then, in an extremely useful review of "sin, sickness, alcoholism, and drug addictions," Clinebell mentions several of a "confusing variety of usages," applied, as he says, now and again to alcoholism and other substance addictions–several of which are not mutually exclusive: 1. "Addictions are the result of personal sin. At no point are they sickness" ["substance addiction begins as the sin of drinking or using drugs, progresses to the greater sin of excessive use (abuse), and ends as a sinful habit"–a view Clinebell attributes to rescue missions]. 2. "Addictions begin as personal sin that results in an obsessive-compulsive disease process called addiction" ["a widely accepted view among clergy from different denominations"]. 3. "Addictions are sicknesses that are caused by the sin of voluntary excessive drinking or drug use" ["This is the official Roman Catholic position. The sin is the sin of excess involved in becoming addicted"]. 4. "Alcoholism and other substance addictions are sicknesses caused by the convergence of a variety of factors involving both sin and sickness, responsibility and compulsivity" ["approximates the view of A.A. . . . a psychological compulsion joined with the physical addiction to alcohol... one is driven to drink by selfishness and its symptoms"]. 5. "Alcoholism and drug dependence involve sin in the sense that they have destructive consequences. These include preventing people from developing their God-given capacities for living fully and productively" ["sin in the sense expressed in the New Testament as 'missing the mark.' . . If sin is defined as anything that harms persons, whatever the cause, then addiction most certainly involves sin"]. 6. "Addictions are illnesses resulting from social sins" ["Our society contributes in many ways to the causes of addictions. It therefore has an inescapable responsibility for both their prevention and treatment"]. 7. "Alcoholism and other addictions involve original sin" ["There often seems to be a certain recalcitrance at the very center of human beings that tends to inhibit doing what we know to be good for ourselves and others. This has been described, in traditional theological language, as the 'bondage of the will.' In even our best acts, we humans seem to have an inescapable self-centeredness that causes us to deify ourselves, our cultures, our religions, institutions, sacred books, the things we make. . . . By making ourselves the center of the universe, we cut ourselves off from our own fulfillment–a fulfillment that is possible only by the self-transcendence that enables us to establish mutually enhancing relationships with other people, the Creator, and the rest of the natural world, God's creation"] (pp. 287-91). Dr. Clinebell tells us a great deal more, also providing a clarification of his own position on the foregoing points. But there is not time here to repeat it here. Further, many of his comments have to do with the opportunities he and we believe are present for the 21st Century–a matter to be discussed later.

My Own Summary of A.A.'s Major Virtues

I'm not very interested in the great applause, and the reasons accompanying it, that author White extends to A.A. White's points seem more likely to justify the continuing referrals to A.A. from treatment centers, therapists, clergy, and courts than they are, or might be, in proving any present-day successes in A.A. In fact, those of us who are active AAs, and those in the treatment community who open their eyes, must almost inevitably affirm the very low success rates in today's A.A. and the tremendous difference between the A.A. of today and the A.A. of the 40 pioneers.

Nor am I intensely enthused over the various definitions of, and proclamations about sin. Or about the Oxford Group's focus on *soul surgery* that would cut away and eliminate sin. I suppose I'm against sin, but I can see the word "sin" driving far more suffering alkies out of A.A. than the alleged possible exodus that is supposed to result from use of the word "God." When most of us enter A.A., we feel like moral lepers; we look like moral lepers; and lots of times we continue to act like moral lepers–lying, stealing, cheating, and all the rest of the things Paul enjoined in the Church epistles. What A.A. certainly does do for those of us who take the program seriously is to call attention to our "sinful" characteristics, behavior, harms, and wrongs–things that most assuredly need substantial change and correction.

I know I won't win any academic or research medals for stating, and probably repeating others in their statements of, the following virtues of A.A. for me personally. But they are compelling, dynamic, personal, and very real:

A.A. Is a Fabulous Time-filler

It is a great time-filler for people who have had more than enough time on their hands, used it foolishly, and gotten into trouble as they did. "Idle hands are the devil's workshop," someone's grandma used to say. And the vacuum that accompanies the long hours of early sobriety is unbelievable. What can I possibly do to avoid loneliness and fear and despair now that I'm not drinking or using? That question is probably on all our minds–at the outset and for quite some time thereafter. And the A.A. answer: "Don't drink, and go to meetings." "Use the telephone." "Get commitments." "Go to meetings early, and leave late." "Go to the meetings after the meetings–for coffee and the like." "Help another drunk." "Stick with the winners; go where they go; do what they do; and you'll get what they've got." "Call your sponsor." "Read the Big Book." "Work the Steps." "Stay away from slippery places and slippery people." Even, "HALT"–don't get too hungry, angry, lonely, or tired." "Don't miss *any* A.A. functions–Conferences, A.A. Roundups, Unity Days, Gratitude Nights, A.A. Retreats, "alkathons," A.A. sobriety birthday parties, A.A. dances, ball games with A.A. members, movies with members; book and Step studies with members , church with members, playing ping pong and pool with members, and hanging out at sober clubs." Do these sound like intellectual pursuits? Not to me, but I did them all. And their value was beyond measure. You substitute A.A. life, viewpoints, and activities for old unworthy or dangerous or immoral or reckless actions that led to or involved drinking. These A.A. ways provide the meandering and lonely newcomer with guides and activities that no jail or judge or drug court or probation officer or correctional system or treatment program or rehab or church group or recovery pastor or government agency can possibly provide. And over a very critical, extended, recovery period. Furthermore, it's all free. There no Dr. Bob, no Anne Smith, no Bible, no God, no Jesus Christ, no gift of the Holy Spirit, no new birth, no Christian Fellowship–yet! Just plain time-filling. And it's all free.

A.A. Offers to the Newcomer Its "Common Solution"

A.A.'s "common solution" requires that the newcomer focus on examining *some* old and "sinful" conduct and ideas, abandoning *some* old and harmful behavior, correcting *some* old and harmful wrongs, learning *and practicing some* widely recognized and accepted religious virtues, passing on those techniques, and helping others to get well. "We are not saints," Bill Wilson tells us. He then adds that we claim spiritual progress rather than spiritual perfection. And that's probably not too shabby a start, provided there is a complete set of standards for truth and moral behavior. "Yardsticks" were what Dr. Bob called the Four Absolutes of the Oxford Group and Pioneer A.A.–Absolute Honesty, Absolute Purity, Absolute Unselfishness, Absolute Love. "Character defects" were what Bill called his version of moral shortcomings members were instructed to remove (with God's help); and these were dishonesty, selfishness, anger, fear, inconsiderate sex conduct, and harmful behavior. Then to substitute patience, tolerance, kindness, love, and service. Eventually, these vices and virtues were standardized into Big Book instructions about dealing with them. But our founder Bill did leave out "fornication" and not only engaged in, but probably spawned a new era of "relationships anonymous." Bill's step standards, however, did provide a discipline for change. One old timer advocated "three D's for recovery"–Decision, Determination, Discipline. And, so long as the standards used were appropriate godly standards, these provided a disciplined substitute for an undisciplined life that had led to destruction.

A.A. Offers an Invitation to Find God and "Do" His Will.

Though the A.A. newcomer may be puzzled by today's meeting babble and endless literature about a "higher power" and unbelief, he is at least introduced very early to the idea that *God has something to do with getting well.* Like so many others in today's fellowships, I had to ignore the irreligious, atheistic, New Age nonsense and phoney "gods" and eventually learned where A.A. had originated. I also had to ignore the Christian-bashing, Bible denouncing, and criticisms of religion that abound in today's meetings. But I can truthfully say that, prior to my A.A. days, I had never related recovery from alcoholism with relying on God and trying to live life His way. Nonetheless, this idea became a cardinal part of my later recovery and deliverance–however well I implemented the principle. It came from increasing return of mental acuity, increasing need for guidance, and increasing awareness that I could obtain my help from Bible study and prayer and, of course, from the Creator. I never regarded A.A. as my religion or the Big Book as my Bible. They were no substitute, and I knew it. If drinking represented "displaced" actions of a healthy nature, I found that acting in accordance with God's will produced the very results that God promised would be forthcoming. The promises were in the Bible itself and in revelations received from God in other ways.

A.A.'s Warmth and Brotherhood

You can get screwed and tattooed in A.A. just as quickly as you can in church, in school, in business, in government, in the military, and in jail. And many have been. There are skunks in A.A. just like there are skunks in the woods. But your very helplessness at the beginning makes you trusting of the hands that are extended, the hugs that occur so frequently, the friendliness and laughter that abound, and the real concern that pops up from unexpected sources at very necessary times. Can you get this elsewhere? Of course, you can. But you probably need it more, expect it less, and receive it in greater measure in A.A. than you do from your church, your doctor, your therapist, your treatment program, your vocational associates, and even–at the beginning–from your family and friends.

A.A. Offers Applause for a Job Well Done

Nothing in early sobriety quite equals the wild cheers, the hearty applause, and the firm back-slapping that goes on at "chip" or "birthday meetings" that celebrate 24 hours, 30 days, 90 days, six months, a year, and beyond, of sobriety. Nothing! Some of us call them "academy award" meetings because of the clamor and enthusiasm that characterize the events. If a cigarette smoker, a sex addict, or a gambler got that much attention for quitting, it might be a far different country today–at least far different from that arising out of tobacco litigation.

Bill Wilson's Genius for Describing the Alcoholic and His Behavior

Bill's own story at the beginning of our Big Book is neither timeless nor a perfect caricature of the alcoholic as far as I am concerned. On the other hand, I'm one of those who believes Bill Wilson was an excellent writer. For example, his descriptions in the early Big Book chapters ("There is a Solution" and "More About Alcoholism") have become legendary and a regular part of our language. There's no need to repeat them here. But every AA knows the expressions "We are like men who have lost their legs." "Here are some of the methods we have tried." And the story of the old boy who was bone-dry for twenty-five years, who retired at the age of fifty-five–and then, "Out came his carpet slippers and a bottle . . . and [he] was dead within four years." The story of "Jim." and his drive in the country, mixing alcohol and milk. The story of the jay-walker who had a passion for skipping in front of fast-moving vehicles. And the conclusion by the "staff member of a world renowned hospital" who said of two alcoholics: "There is no doubt in my mind that you were 100% hopeless, apart from divine help." Whether we accept, and proceed to implement, Wilson's points or not, his descriptions stick with us, amuse us, are oft-repeated in the Fellowship, and can be unbelievably useful if learned.

3

The Good News
What God Can Do about Alcoholism

You (the "Party of the First Part")
Need Pioneer Understanding of God

I myself will never adopt an understanding that *the power* to overcome "disease" or "sin" or "sickness" or whatever alcoholism is, can be received from, or operated with, "something" or "somebody" or a "power greater than myself" or a "higher power" or a "group" or a lightbulb, chair, bulldozer, goddess, doorknob, radiator or any of the other "absurd names for God" (as Rev. Sam Shoemaker, our "co-founder" described them). I wouldn't rely on a "Something." I wouldn't trust a "Somebody." I wouldn't seek help from "a higher power." [Some in A.A. say they will only settle for the "Highest Power"–Almighty God]. I wouldn't pray to a group. And I certainly wouldn't expect guidance from a lightbulb, healing by a doorknob, deliverance in the seat of a chair, or forgiveness through the accomplishments of a radiator.

A.A.'s Big Book has always said, and still says, there is One with all power and that the One is God! The founders used all kinds of descriptions and titles for God–Father, Creator, Maker, Almighty God–but they all came from the Good Book. That understanding of God produced a 75% to 93% early A.A. success rate in our earliest groups. And it produced a new life and new happiness for me.

You Need the Pioneers' Belief That God Can Heal You

The founders believed the Bible. It says that God can cure, heal, and deliver. It says that Jesus Christ made that power available to all who believe [John 14:12: "Verily, verily, I say unto you, He that believeth on me, the works that I do shall he do also; and greater *works* than these shall he do; because I go unto my Father." Acts 1:5, 8: "For John truly baptized with water; but ye shall be baptized with the Holy Ghost not many days hence. . . . But ye shall receive power, after that the Holy Ghost is come upon you: and ye shall be witnesses unto me both in Jerusalem, and in all Judaea, and in Samaria, and unto the uttermost part of the earth."]. Some in the A.A. publishing game of today have taken to promoting the idea that those words–cure, healing, and deliverance–were misleading and, by their interpretations, were mistaken. Are they saying the *Bible* is misleading and mistaken? I don't think so. There was a safer and less controversial course for them to take. The safest way for those who promulgate the "there-must-have-been-a-mistake-in-the-language-used" propaganda was simply to eliminate the language from A.A. usage. No "cure." No "ex-alcoholics." Just create a diversion, and abrogate mention of the Bible. Add some new names for God, even though they describe some incomprehensible and non-existent idol. Delete all reference to Jesus Christ. Stop writing about early A.A.'s spiritual roots and history. And just call our A.A. fellowship a "self-help" mutual hand-holding society with love and good works as its basic tenets. Safe, but pretty sorry!

The problem in letting the ubiquitous revisionists get away with such desecrations of our pioneer program is that they are dealing with alcoholism. Alcoholism is devastating. It is destructive. It is dangerous. It is corrupting. It is not a problem to be left in the hands of some virtually self-appointed, unaccountable publishing committee in New York or teams of writers who may not have seen or helped a "wet drunk" in years. Nor is alcoholism a problem to be left to group therapy. Liver disease doesn't yield either to group therapy or newly published names. The numbness in my legs was not receptive to "self-help." My seizures did not abate with hugs. My fear and terror did not disappear by sitting in a chair at an A.A. meeting. In fact, many in A.A. still say that their arch-enemy (Self-centeredness) is so difficult to overcome that it has to be "crucified" just as Jesus was crucified. Again, the Good Book says quite clearly that God can cure, heal, and deliver. In early A.A., the Pioneers said over and over that God had done, or was doing, for them what they could not do for themselves. Then, in his own first-published effort, Bill Wilson made a new, unwarranted, and bald-faced insertion. He added to his A.A. of 1939 the statement that alcoholism cannot be cured. But that was not the picture the founders first painted.

The "No Cure" Crowd. Yet it became a watchword for professionals–no cure! Vernon E. Johnson plastered "hopelessness" and "treatment" all over the professional scene:

> You are a patient in this two-year treatment program because you are sick with a chronic addiction–that is, a harmful dependency on a chemical substance which interferes with your daily life. **Because your condition is chronic, you cannot be cured**. But you can be treated successfully [Vernon E. Johnson. *I'll Quit Tomorrow: A Practical guide to the alcoholism treatment which has worked for seven out of ten exposed to the Johnson Institute approach* [New York: Harper and Row, 1973], p. 113; bold face added).

> *Is Alcoholism a Disease?* Yes, because one's addiction to chemicals is uncontrollable and unpredicted. Alcoholism is an illness that one does not go out to look for or buy. It just happens. **One frustrating thing is that alcoholism cannot be cured** (Johnson, *I'll Quit Tomorrow*, p. 159; bold face added).

Vernon Johnson founded the Johnson Institute in 1966 after he had received his Bachelor of Divinity and Doctor of Divinity from Seabury Western Theological Seminary in Illinois. What happened to God? Now, let's see what happened to "no cure" and "treatment."

The "Relapse Is OK" Crowd. The fact is that, with the word "relapse" added to make things sound OK, the "no cure–treatment–relapse" disorder became a sump-hole for millions upon millions of dollars in public and private expenditures. And it still is. Consider the following statement in a recent U.S. government pamphlet:

> Addiction is a progressive, chronic, primary, relapsing disorder. It generally involves compulsion, loss of control, and continued use of alcohol and other drugs despite adverse consequences. Addiction, treatment, recovery, and relapse are all dynamic biopsychosocial processes (Mim J. Landry. *Overview of Addiction Treatment Effectiveness* [Rockville, MD: Substance Abuse and Mental Health Services Administration, Office of Applied Studies. Revised February, 1997], p. iii).

> Many people mistakenly believe that relapse is a sign of treatment failure. Early models of addiction viewed successful treatment and relapse as "all-or-nothing." Today, both treatment and relapse are understood to be dynamic processes. In particular, relapse is viewed as a transitional process from abstinence to active addiction. The relapse process consists of a series of events and changes in thinking, attitude, behavior–that may or may not be followed by the use of substances. Even if use resumes, it may not reach the same level of intensity as before treatment–at least for a while (Landry, *Overview of Addiction Treatment Effectiveness*, p. 62).

This prompts me to wonder if author Landry believes that the alcoholic's plight is much like "being a little pregnant" as he approaches this "dynamic process." Take God out of the picture, and you may wish to consider the very "lack of defense" and "lack of power" that prompted AAs to say that it meant, "of course," that they were going to talk about God!

We've already quoted just a few of the **Bible verses that point to God's ability and willingness to heal, cure, deliver, and assure**

that we overcome. Pioneer AAs had ready access to these verses, not only in their own Bibles, but also in *The Runner's Bible* they used so frequently.

A.A. Pioneers Talked about "Cure"

A.A.'s own Conference Approved literature quotes clear remarks by Bill Wilson, by Dr. Bob Smith, and by Bill Dotson–A.A.'s number 1, 2, and 3–on their being cured of alcoholism. They are explicit about their cure and the source of the cure–God:

> "Says Bill W.: Nineteen years ago last summer, Dr. Bob saw him (Bill D.) for the first time. Two days before this, Dr. Bob had said to me, 'If you and I are going to stay sober, we had better get busy.' **Straightaway, Bob called Akron's City Hospital** and asked for the nurse on the receiving ward. **He [Dr. Bob] explained that he [Dr. Bob] and a man from New York [Bill Wilson] had a cure for alcoholism**" (*Alcoholics Anonymous*, 3rd ed., p. 188; bold face added; *DR. BOB and the Good Oldtimers*, pp. 81-82).

> Bill D. (The lawyer Bill Dotson) said: "It was in the next two or three days after I had first met Doc and Bill, that I finally came to a decision to turn my will over to God and to go along with the program the best I could. . . . I did come to the conclusion that I was willing to put everything I had into it, **with God's power**, and that I wanted to do just that. As soon as I had done that I did feel a great release. I knew that I had a helper that I could rely upon, who wouldn't fail me. If I could stick to Him and listen, I would make it" (*Alcoholics Anonymous,* 3rd ed., pp. 188-90; bold face added).

> Bill Wilson said of a later visit in the next day or so to Bill Dotson at the hospital "Before our visit was over, Bill [Dotson] turned to his wife and said, 'Go fetch my clothes, dear. We're going to get up and get out of here.' **Bill D. walked out of that hospital a free man never to drink again. A.A.'s Number One**

Group dates from that very day" (*Alcoholics Anonymous*, 3rd ed., p. 189; bold face added).

Then, after Dotson had been home from the hospital for about two weeks, Dotson reported (in his personal Big Book story) the following conversation among Dotson, Dotson's wife Henrietta, and Bill Wilson: "Bill [Wilson] was over to my house talking to my wife and me. We were eating lunch, and I was listening and trying to find out why they [Dr. Bob and Bill Wilson] had this release that they seemed to have. **Bill [Wilson] looked across at my wife, and said to her, 'Henrietta, the Lord has been so wonderful to me, curing me of this terrible disease**, that I just want to keep talking about it and telling people.' I [Bill Dotson] thought, 'I think I have the answer.' Bill [Wilson] was very, very grateful that he had been released from this terrible thing and he had given God the credit for having done it, and he's so grateful about it he wants to tell other people about it. **That sentence, 'The Lord has been so wonderful to me, curing me of this terrible disease, that I just want to keep telling people about it,' has been a sort of golden text for the A.A. program and for me** [Bill Dotson]" (*Alcoholics Anonymous*, 3rd ed., p. 191; see also *DR. BOB and the Good Oldtimers*, p. 83; and Dick B., *The Golden Text of A.A.: God, the Pioneers, and Real Spirituality* [Kihei, HI: Paradise Research Publications, 1999], pp. 9, 55-61; bold face added).

Wilson again chose to speak of a cure, when he interviewed T. Henry and Clarace Williams in 1954. Wilson said:

God knows we've been simple enough and gluttonous enough to get this way, but once we got this way [became alcoholics], **it was a form of lunacy which only God Almighty could cure** (Dick B., *The Akron Genesis of Alcoholics*, 2d ed. [Kihei, HI: Paradise Research Publications, 1998], p. 13; bold face added).

While we cannot specifically attribute the cover draft to Bill Wilson himself, one of the early proposed covers for the First Edition of *Alcoholics Anonymous* touted A.A. as a "cure" for alcoholism.

Pioneer Clarence H. Snyder reiterated the early A.A. beliefs of his colleagues (Bill W., Dr. Bob, and Bill Dotson) as to their cure by the "Great Physician." See the repeated use of the "cure" term in Mitchell K. *How It Worked: The Story of Clarence H. Snyder and the Early Days of Alcoholics Anonymous in Cleveland Ohio* (NY: AA Big Book Study Group, 1997), pp. 6, 71, 138, 157, 235; and the "Great Physician" reference to Jesus Christ was in common use among other Pioneer AAs, by their New York mentor Dr. Silkworth, and their Oxford Group friends. See, for example, H. A. Walter, *Soul Surgery* (Oxford: Printed at the University Press, 1932), p. 4.

William D. Silkworth, M.D., and the Charles B. Towns Hospital may or may not have disagreed as to whether alcoholism could be cured. Charles B. Towns was the owner of Towns Hospital, where Bill Wilson had his "spiritual experience" while under the care of Towns' medical director, Dr. William Silkworth. Towns had claimed to have a "cure" for alcoholism. Dr. Silkworth, on the other hand, said, "clinically, we have no cure for chronic alcoholism. . . . The disease was merely arrested." Nonetheless, it was Silkworth who was responsible for the following positions: (1) Urging clergy and men of religion to renew or revive the practice of prayer, particularly meditation; (2) Distinguishing between the use of alcohol which does not produce a chronic alcoholic and that in which there is "the allergic nature of true alcoholism"; (3) Stressing that "elimination of the phenomenon of craving that follows the treatment does not constitute a cure [but that] the final cure rests with themselves [alcoholics in the second phase of alcoholism]"; (4) Advocating "moral psychology" in achieving entire recovery from alcoholism; (5) Describing the success of the A.A. spiritual approach as requiring the patient's willingness to turn his life and his problems over to the care and direction of his Creator; (6) Applauding the A.A. plan to make a "so-called transfer to one greater than themselves, to God"; (7) Urging Bill Wilson to hang on to his spiritual experience; and (8) Having told a parishioner of the famous Dr. Norman Vincent Peale that the parishioner/alcoholic named Chuck could be healed by the Great Physician Jesus Christ. (The preceding remarks by Dr. Silkworth can be found in the series of articles sent to the present author via email titled "William Duncan Silkworth, M.D., Some Writings by & about 'The Little Doctor Who Loved Drunks'" from Mary H. on April 11, 2002. See also Norman Vincent Peale, *The Positive Power of Jesus Christ*.)

The Founders Were Not Alone in Their Faith That God Cures Alcoholism

God Is for the Alcoholic

In *God Is for the Alcoholic*, Jerry Dunn writes: Alcoholism is a sickness of the soul–a sin sickness, and it must be considered such (p. 21). When the alcoholic is at the bottom and has come to the place where he doesn't want to take another drink, then we can help him to break the cycle. The cycle can be broken. We can thank God for that. He has provided a way of escape. . . the way we will be able to help the alcoholic to break the cycle and overcome addiction. It is possible for him to be completely free from the power of alcohol addiction (p. 55). I have dealt with men who were chronic alcoholics for many years. Yet I have never seen a man who has honestly and sincerely confessed his sin and turned his life completely to God who hasn't been delivered from the power of beverage alcohol. Yes, God was for me. He is for you. God is for the alcoholic (p. 162).

Dr. Bob's Special Emphasis on Christian Healing

There were two very powerful Christian healing titles among the many on that subject which were owned, studied, and circulated among A.A. pioneers by Dr. Bob. (See Dick B., *Dr. Bob and His Library*, 3rd ed. [Kihei, HI: Paradise Research Publications, 1998].) I've seen, studied, and listed all these titles, and the following two are extremely useful in telling us what we can do, just as the early AAs did.

Heal the Sick. The first—*Heal the Sick*—is a 277-page, fine print, book by an Episcopal layman and student who spent twenty-four years in "Christian Healing" which culminated in five years' world-wide Healing Mission. The title is *Heal the Sick* by **James Moore Hickson** (London: Methuen & Co., Ltd., 1924). The book details literally thousands of healings all over the world that were attested by clergy and others. Hickson rejects the idea that the "age of miracles is now past," that "There is no need for Christian Healing in these days of enlightenment and advance in medical and surgical science," and that "doctors and surgeons," as "healing servants of God constitute (the only way) by which God's healing comes to us" (p. 3). Emphatically he says, "To understand the full significance of Christian Healing we must think spiritually, we must approach the subject on the spiritual plane, and we must remember that it is healing through the Person and Power of Jesus Christ, and Him alone" (p. 2). Hickson documented his assertion with specific cases: Complete cures were claimed as to pain, rheumatism, ear discharge, goitre, severe headaches, and blood poisoning (p. 118); blindness, paralysis, deafness, possession by evil spirits, asthma, stammering, and curvature of the spine (p. 128); palsy, dumbness, and mental deficiency (p. 151); deformed feet and legs made almost entirely normal (p. 152); "the healing of sin-sick souls" and "the healing of the body" (p. 168); partial paralysis, paralysis, infantile paralysis, rheumatoid arthritis, neuritis, St. Vitus's dance, epilepsy, and mental disorders (pp. 182-183)." Hickson quotes a Bishops Pastoral Letter, addressed to the people of the Church of England in Australia, signed by all the archbishops and bishops in whose dioceses the Healing Missions were held. The clergy attested to "spiritual forces at work–the response of a loving Father to the prayer of His children, the healing power of a present Saviour, the renewing influence of the Holy Spirit upon spirit, mind, and body" (pp. 198-199). They concluded that three things were needed in preparing congregations to assist the Ministry of Healing: (1) *Penitence*–the desire to be healed of all that is sinful in heart and life, all disobedience to the Will of God, all doubt of His love, all bitter and unloving thoughts of others. Only a penitent soul can expect to be healed. (2) *Faith*–God is working for the redemption of soul and body. God's primary purpose for His children is holiness and health. (3) *Prayer*–True faith finds expression in prayer; it is not faith alone, but the prayer of faith that is the human condition of Divine Healing (p. 202). Hickson urges recognition of the following four things: (1) The appalling amount of physical, mental, and spiritual suffering there is in the world, which lies beyond the help of man; and hence the great need of the Healing Saviour. (2) The wonderful faith of the people, their readiness to step out in the Name of Jesus Christ, and their desire to be led by the Church. (3) That the time is ripe for the revival in the Church of the Ministry of Healing. (4) How incomplete and inadequate the Church's Ministry is, and also that of Medical Science, without the use of the spiritual gifts and powers, with which the Church is endowed; and the need for closer cooperation of doctor and priest in the work under Christ, the Healing Saviour, for the full and complete redemption and healing of the bodies and souls of men. He adds: "The Church is working mainly for the soul's salvation, the medical profession is trying to stamp out disease, Christ is the Great Physician of the body, and the Saviour of the soul. His work was and is, to give full and complete redemption to man's whole being, and to fit us for the Kingdom of God. If the world is to be freed from sickness and suffering, it must be free from sin–the root case of all disorder, physical, mental and spiritual–and the starting point is repentance. When man's heart is changed, the world will be changed. Then the one prayer will be: "THY KINGDOM COME, THY WILL BE DONE ON EARTH AS IT IS IN HEAVEN" . . . And if the victory is to be won, it will be by the power of Christ through man, for there is no other Name under Heaven by which we can receive health and salvation, but only the name of Jesus Christ" (pp. 238-239). The author's final chapters lay great stress on the work of the Holy Spirit in Christian healing; and many of the verses from the Bible that early AAs studied can be found cited by Hickson in these chapters–verses from the Gospels, from Acts, from James, from Corinthians, from Ephesians–and others dealing with the "gifts of healing." (See 1 Corinthians 12:9.)

Healing in Jesus Name: The second significant title on healing that Dr. Bob studied and circulated—*Healing in Jesus Name*—is one I recommend for all those who desire to know what the founders investigated concerning their "cure" by the power of God. It is *Healing in Jesus Name: Fifteen Sermons and Addresses on Salvation and Healing*, by **Ethel R. Willitts** (Detroit, Michigan: Ethel R. Willitts, Evangelist, 1931). Sister Willitts refers to a large number of healings she brought about. But she also lays out the brick and mortar of Christian healing. And it comes from Bible verses that were commonplace in early A.A. literature. Some of Willitts's compelling chapter titles are: (1) The Will of God. (2) Whom Does the Lord Heal. (3) Stumbling Blocks to Faith. (4) Fear Not–the Deliverer is at Hand. (5) Because of Your Unbelief. (6) Completeness in Christ. (7) Faith–What It Is–How it is Obtained. (8) The Double Cure–Salvation and Healing. (9) Facts on Miracles and Healings of Today. (10) Does God Need the Aid of Medicine in Healing. I will not attempt to detail all of Willitts's points, but she adds great force to her approach by relying on Bible verses which are relevant to the subject, well-known, and widely mentioned. She says, "Christ said that salvation was a fact, and we know His healing and miracles were a fact" (p. 10); and she covers both Old and New Testament healing accounts. Answering a point so often raised in A.A. meetings today as to the will of God, she points out that healing has to do with the will and promises of God: "When the Lord promises to heal our bodies of any disease, He will do just what he says he will do. . . . The apostles in the early church times knew the will of God–that the sick and suffering were to have prayer offered for them, and that the Lord would cure their diseases" (p. 26). "Divine healing has all of heaven's endorsements" (p. 36). "Whom does the Lord heal? Will He heal all the people that come unto Him? Is He the same mighty Christ that He was when He walked on earth as man? Yes!" (p. 41) "He quickens those that are dead in trespasses and sin and heals the body" (p. 47). "How different were the diseases of people who thronged about Christ to be healed . . . . All who reached Him were healed" (p. 48). "There are two streams flowing from Calvary–salvation and healing; but you must come to the meeting place–Christ–believe in Him and confess Him as your Lord" (p. 52). She lists stumbling blocks to faith such as failing to call on elders of the church (James 5:14); disobedience (1 Peter 2:8); "unclean lips"–"They which preach the gospel should live of the gospel" with a heart full of compassion and love for one another" (Mark 11:25); "Sickness, or afflictions on your body, will not become as a fear to you if you are saved and know Christ as the Great Physician. . . . When Jesus Christ died on Calvary, He died there to destroy all sin and sin's effects. Sickness and disease are the effect of sin. In Christ lie the supplies of health and life eternal. Why let unbelief, or an unforgiving spirit, or what people say of sin, stand in your way as a stumbling block. . . . turn a deaf ear to unbelievers" (p. 66). You must have Active faith–an instantaneous faith that takes the promise now (p. 70). There are many many Biblical positions she urges: Becoming born again. Believing the Bible. Knowing that we can be made complete in soul and body–a complete salvation and a complete healing in Jesus Christ (Colossians 2:9-10). There is no case too hard for Jesus. We have been delivered from the power of darkness (Colossians 1:13). Jesus came to save and heal; and he bore all our sins and sickness (Isaiah 53:5; 1 Peter 2:24). Make a complete surrender. Whatever your needs be, do not stop until you have come to Christ and are delivered, whether it be from sin in your soul or from sickness in your body (p.159). Bible reading and prayer are essential!

Dr. Bob's Many Other Books
on Healing and the Power of Prayer

There were many other powerful attestations in Dr. Bob's library to specific cure and healing of mind and body by the power of God. Dr. Bob especially admired **Glenn Clark**, owned and circulated his healing book, and even attended his prayer camp with his (Dr. Bob's) wife, Anne. Clark's healing title was *How to Find Health through Prayer*, 3rd ed.(New York: Harper & Brothers, 1940). And there were many others by authors of several of persuasions, most pointing up the accomplishments of Jesus Christ. These were: *Parish the Healer* by Maurice Barbanell (London: Psychic Book Club, 1938); *Life*

Abundant for You by Louis Brownell (CA: The Aquarian Ministry, 1928); *Handles of Power* by Lewis L. Dunnington (New York: Abingdon-Cokesbury Press, 1942; *Science and Health with Key to the Scriptures* by Mary Baker Eddy (Boston: Published by the Trustees under the Will of Mary Baker G. Eddy, n.d.); *Christian Healing* by Charles Fillmore (Missouri: Unity School of Christianity, n.d.); *The Meaning of Prayer* by Harry Emerson Fosdick (New York: Association Press, 1915); *Quiet Talks on Prayer* by S. D. Gordon (London: Fleming, n.d.); *The Runner's Bible: Spiritual Guidance for People on the Run* by Nora Smith Holm (Colorado: First Acropolis Book Edition, 1998); *Recovery* by Starr Daily (St. Paul: Macalester Park Publishing Company, 1948); *Getting Results by Prayer* by Emmet Fox (1933); *Power Through Constructive Thinking*, 12th ed., by Emmet Fox (New York: Harper & Brothers, 1940); **A Preface to Prayer** by Gerald Heard (New York: Harper & Brothers, 1944); *Prayer (Mightiest Force in the World)* by Frank Laubach (New York: Fleming H. Revell, 1946); *Victorious Living* by E. Stanley Jones (New York: Abingdon Press, 1936); *A Primer of Prayer* by Charles Laymon (Nashville: Tidings, 1949); *Perfect Everything* by Rufus Mosely (St. Paul: Macalester Publishing Company, 1949); *Prayer Can Change Your Life* by Dr. William R. Parker and Elaine St. Johns, new ed. (NY: Prentice Hall, 1957); *The Nature of True Prayer* by F. L. Rawson (England: The Society for Spreading the Knowledge of True Prayer, 1918); *Creative Prayer* by E. Herman (London: James Clarke & Co., circa 1921); and probably Elwood Worcester, Samuel McComb, Isador H. Coriat. *Religion and Medicine: The Moral Control of Nervous Disorders* (New York: Moffat, Yard & Company, 1908).

The Power of God in Healing–even of the Alcoholic!

Some Good Old Testimonials

First, some dramatic testimony which matches the healings of early A.A.

The lawyer: The lawyer was a "heavy drinker" and, in confessing his "weakness," he expressed a belief that there was "something in the Bible that says no drunkard shall have any part in the kingdom of God." His Christian friend then drew close to the lawyer, read him some portions of the Bible, and said, "Let us get down and pray." The lawyer prayed a simple prayer expressing his new faith in Christ and requesting that the power of alcohol would be broken in his life. Later, speaking of his deliverance from alcohol, the converted lawyer said, "Put it down big, put it down plain, that God broke that power instantly." The lawyer's name was C. I. Scofield, known now to millions as the editor of the Scofield Reference Bible. His faith in Christ freed him from the enslaving power of alcohol (Van Impe, *Alcohol: The Beloved Enemy*, pp. 156-57).

R.H.R.: "When I came to the Harbor Light [a Salvation Army facility] back in 1958, I was broken and defeated in many ways: mentally, spiritually and physically. At that point I turned my life over to God, and asked Him to help me. He answered my prayers, and now, with 8 years of sobriety back of me, thanks to His grace, I am and have for some time enjoyed a peace of mind that I had never before experienced. I read my Bible often, and do my best to live a good Christian life" (Van Impe, *Alcoholism: The Total Treatment Approach*, p. 358).

E.L.W.: When he finally arrived at Harbor Light, a derelict, he related that he had, during the preceding 10 years, been arrested over 100 times and had spent the greater part of this time in prisons. . . . He had tried hospital programs, dry-out centers, faith healing, cures and alcoholic programs–but without success. . . . Upon enrollment he did exceptionally well with us right from the beginning, and within 10 days gave testimony of having received a spiritual rebirth. He was elected by his fellows as chaplain of the men's fellowship club and showed, in every facet of his life, a dramatic change. . . . This man became a Salvationist in December, 1965, and gives a forthright testimony to the power of God in his life (Van Impe, *Alcoholism: The Total Treatment Approach*, pp. 356-57).

Some Representative Advocates of Healing

The following are neither representative of all, nor a comprehensive list of, nor the totality of, the writings and views of thousands who believe and/or confirm, from one starting point or another, that the healing power of Jesus Christ is available today: Norman Vincent Peale, *The Positive Power of Jesus Christ: Life-changing Adventures in Faith* (Carmel, NY: Guideposts, 1980); Philip Yancey, *What's So Amazing about Grace?* (Grand Rapids, MI: Zondervan, 1997); E. W. Kenyon, *In His Presence: The Secret of Prayer* (Kenyon Publishing Society, 1999); E. W. Kenyon, *Jesus the Healer* (Kenyon Gospel Publishing Society, 2000); E. W. Kenyon, *The Hidden Man* (WA: Kenyon Publishing Society, 1998); E. W. Kenyon, *The Wonderful Name of Jesus* (Kenyon's Gospel Publishing Society, 1998); John Baker, *Celebrate Recovery* (CA: Celebrate Recovery Books, 1994); Bob and Pauline Bartosch, *Overcomers Outreach: A Bridge to Recovery* (La Habra, CA: Overcomers Outreach, 1994); Cathy Burns, *Alcoholics Anonymous Unmasked* (PA: Sharing, 1991); Cal Chambers, *Two Tracks-One Goal* (British Columbia: Credo Publishing Corporation, 1992); Martin M. Davis, *The Gospel and the Twelve Steps* (San Diego, CA: RPI Publishing Inc., 1993); Len C. Freeland, author of Chapter 28, "The Salvation Army" in *Alcoholism: The Total Treatment Approach*, edited by Ronald J. Catanzaro (IL: Charles C. Thomas Publisher, 1968); Mark H. Graeser, John A. Lynn, John W. Schoenheit, *Don't Blame God: A Biblical Answer to the Problem of Evil, Sin and Suffering.* (Indianapolis: Christian Educational Services, 1994); J. Keith Miller, *A Hunger for Healing* (NY: HarperCollins Publishers, 1991); William L. Playfair, *The Useful Lie* (Wheaton, IL: Crossway Books, 1991); John R. Cheydleur, *Every Day Sober is a Miracle* (Wheaton, IL: Tyndale House Publishers, Inc., 1996); Saul Selby, *Twelve Step Christianity* (MN: Hazelden, 2000); Loren Cunningham, *Is That Really You, God?: Hearing the Voice of God* (Seattle: YWAM Publishing, 1984); Nora Smith Holm, *The Runner's Bible: Spiritual Guidance for People on the Run* (GA: Acropolis Books, , 1st ed., 1998); Jim Wallis, *Faith Works: Lessons from the Life of an Activist*

Preacher (New York: Random House, 2000); Anderson Spickard and Barbara R. Thompson, ***Dying for a Drink*** (Waco, TX: Word Book Publishers, 1985); Edward E. Decker, Jr, "**'Praying Through'**: A Pentecostal Approach to Pastoral Care." *Journal of Psychology and Christianity* (2001, Vol. 20, No. 4), pp. 370-77.

Defining the Role of God, the Bible, the Church, and the Clergy in Dealing with Alcoholism

Many in the religious community are actively and positively involved in trying to define the proper role of God, the Bible, the Church, and the Clergy in combating alcoholism. Many of those efforts, however, seem timid in terms of real power of God to *cure.* My own view is much more assertive and positive: God can empower, cure, heal, forgive, and deliver. And the religious community can and should do more to foster that conviction. It can teach the Bible. It can vitalize prayer. It can espouse God's guidance. It can minister healing if it uses the tools Jesus Christ made available. Consider this account from Acts 3:

> Now Peter and John went up together into the temple at the hour of prayer, *being* the ninth *hour.*
> And a certain man lame from his mother's womb was carried, whom they laid daily at the gate of the temple which is called Beautiful, to ask alms of them that entered into the temple;
> Who seeing Peter and John about to go into the temple asked an alms.
> And Peter, fastening his eyes upon him with John, said, Look on us.
> And he gave heed unto them, expecting to receive something of them.
> Then Peter said, Silver and gold have I none; but such as I have give I thee: In the name of Jesus Christ of Nazareth rise up and walk.
> And he took him by the right hand, and lifted him up; and immediately his feet and ankle bones received strength.

And he leaping up stood, and walked, and entered with them into the temple, walking, and leaping, and praising God (Acts 3:1-8).

Rev. Sam Shoemaker offered some clear advice. Just look at what A.A.'s "co-founder" and "spiritual well-spring" Rev. Sam Shoemaker wrote about God and the power He makes available to his children–the power even to be delivered from the fears and troubles that accompany alcoholism:

> This kind of power is, I repeat, an achievement of faith, not an endowment of nature. The end result is to be "the sons of God" [1 John 3:2: "Beloved, now are we the sons of God . . ."; 1 John 5:1: "Whosoever believeth that Jesus is the Christ is born of God. . . ."; 1 John 5:4: "For whatsoever is born of God overcometh the world . . ."]. But the prior condition is the reception of "power." We in our day are very familiar with two kinds of power, mechanical power such as you see in dynamos and turbines. . . and then the human power that gathers in great industrial combinations. . . . We know these two kinds of power, mechanical and human. But the New Testament refers to another kind of power. . . . St. John says by implication that this power is not found in men naturally; it is bestowed upon them by grace. There comes upon them a power from without which links up with a power that is within. . . it is the kind of power that is truly and fully found only in God. Until you have seen this power in human lives, you do not understand what the Christian religion is. . . . There He stands, waiting to give us His whole abundant life. It is for them that "receive Him," and no one else can possibly have it. The locks and bars are not on the long gone inn of Bethlehem; there are on our own hearts. We sing it, but we must learn to pray it and mean it (**Samuel M. Shoemaker**, "Power to Become," *The Evangel* [New York: 61 Gramercy Place, December 1954], pp. 40-43; see also John 1:12, which is the subject of Sam's article; and Dick B. *New Light on Alcoholism: God, Sam Shoemaker, and A.A.*, 2d ed. [Kihei, HI: Paradise Research Publications, 1999], pp. 503-17).

The Clinebell Study

If you want a thorough review of the place religion occupies in alcoholism recovery, I feel Dr. Howard Clinebell has done the job best in his ***Understanding and Counseling Persons with Alcohol, Drug, and Behavioral Addictions, supra.*** He covers the definitions of alcoholism and addiction. He covers the A.A. picture and compares that with a good many other treatment "solutions." He sets forth an evaluation of A.A.'s effectiveness. He deals with the sin questions. And he deals with counseling. But there are several points that deserve special emphasis here: (1) "The radical new view of alcoholism, not as a disease but as a 'central activity in heavy drinkers' way of life,' as described by Herbert Fingarette. . . clearly has transforming implications for conceptualizing and dealing with the ethical issues in alcohol addiction. . . . This will occur if the behavioral approaches by which problem drinkers (as believed by those who subscribe to this understanding) can change their drinking-centered way of life, are shown to be widely effective. This could help many more problem drinkers and alcoholics who do not find either A.A. or mainstream disease model treatment center approaches helpful. . . . As Fingarette writes, 'All the newer approaches also emphasize [like current mainstream approaches] that the drinker must accept responsibility and play an active role in bringing about the desired change.' Yale scientist Giorgio Lolli said: 'What is already known breeds a more tolerant attitude toward him [the addictive drinker] and favors a shift of attention from his objectionable deeds to those unfortunate experiences that determined them. The moral issue is not denied but reinterpreted in the light of medical, psychiatric and sociological facts. This reinterpretation helps considerably in efforts to free the addict from his ties to alcohol' (pp. 299-300). Clinebell has some guarded views on how clergy should use religious resources such as prayer, scripture, or sacraments in counseling (p. 390). These may be valid, considering his prestige and experience, but they don't satisfy me as to what the clergy of today need to emphasize and reintroduce—in the same forceful way Rev. Sam Shoemaker introduced them in the 1930's in his books, sermons, talks, and work with Bill Wilson. On the other hand, Clinebell quotes physician Anderson Spickard, medical director of the Vanderbilt University Institute for the Treatment of Addiction: "In my twenty years of medical practice, few experiences have had a resurrection quality equal to that of watching alcoholics and their families leave behind the living death of addiction. Today, while much of the world staggers under the weight of chemical addiction, the church is called upon to be a vessel of this resurrection. . . . With a small investment of time and effort, any church can equip itself to minister to alcoholics and their families. . . . Recovering alcoholics are among the most spiritually vibrant Christians I know, and the enthusiasm and commitment they bring to their relationship with Christ contribute greatly to the spiritual health of the churches they attend" (pp. 433-34).

The Good News

If alcoholism is a disease, God can cure it if a believer seeks Him, asks Him, and obeys Him. If alcoholism is a behavior disorder, a believer who has been freed from bondage can change his behavior with the guidance and power of God. If alcoholism is a nutritional problem, God can certainly fit in that picture, as well as healing everything else that is produced by the problem, if the believer chooses to seek His help. If alcoholism is a sin, a believer can confess that sin, receive forgiveness, elect to turn from that sin, use the power of God in the effort, and end the sinful action by obeying God. (see 1 John 1:5-2:6; Acts 2:38-40). This is certainly not a treatise on how God heals and effects miracles. It is a proclamation as to His availability and power. In Acts 3, the lame man believed, Peter—using the power available after Pentecost—simply commanded in the name of Jesus Christ, and the healing was instantaneous. The Book of Acts is filled with similar examples. Once a person has accepted Christ, there are ample testimonies–some in this book–to God's answering simple prayers by penitent alcoholics. Harold Begbie's *Twice Born Men* (NY: Fleming H. Revell, 1909) contained testimonials written long before A.A. began and of great popularity in Pioneer A.A. Anne Smith specifically lists six such books in her spiritual journal that was shared with early AAs. There's much much more, and this is just an opening challenge.

What Is Not Required in Order to Tell the Good News

One does not have to evangelize A.A., reform it, or convert it to its old-school Christian fellowship form, in order to tell the good news. Old-school A.A. was a Christian Fellowship, studied the Bible, learned about and understood the Creator, came to Him through accepting Jesus Christ, and was blessed with tremendous success by relying on the Creator (or "Heavenly Father").

The successes through this approach are no less available today than they were in the First Century Christian Fellowship of the Bible, in the healing ministries Dr. Bob studied, and in the simple approaches of Akron Number One.

In today's "inclusive" A.A. Fellowship, there should be no hesitancy whatever about telling the truth of A.A.'s early history. There should be no hesitancy whatever about allowing individuals and groups to follow the very practices that were followed in Akron Number One. There should be no banning of Bibles, no bashing of Christians, and no ridiculing of religion–anyone's religion. There should be no hesitancy about encouraging attendance at churches, Bible fellowships, religious retreats, and religious convocations–just as early A.A. did, in Akron and in New York. There should be no hesitancy about putting an end to the observable attempts in word and deed to reform A.A.–to transform it into a fellowship which attempts to attract by down-grading the importance of God and religion and applauds beliefs in idols or anything or nothing at all. There should be no hesitancy about encouraging people to obtain all the help they can get from medicine, from religion, from churches, from rabbis, from ministers, and from priests–just as early A.A. did.

If ever there were a time in A.A.'s short history that it should look at its own early spiritual program, that time is now. The founders are dead. The real spiritual roots–coming directly from the Bible–have been buried and ignored. Probably most AAs have never heard of Frank Amos or the Alcoholic Foundation or the Amos Report. Yet all these embraced and applauded the original program. You don't have to adopt the Pioneer program in order to allow it to be learned within A.A., practiced within A.A., published by A.A., and publicized as one of the important elements of A.A.'s success. These facts should become just as available to anyone anywhere and from A.A. as are A.A.'s Big Book, the Twelve Steps, the Twelve Traditions, and any other resources of this unique and well-known society.

4

The Nonsense "gods" of Recovery

Let's Begin with Some Definitions

For God is not *the author* of confusion, but of peace, as in all churches of the saints (1 Corinthians 14:33).

The Creator

The Pioneer AAs in Akron Number One were looking for a way to end their drinking problem and the woes that seemed the inevitable result thereof. Their founders (Bill Wilson and Dr. Bob) turned to God for the answer–for the "way out." But what God? The answer, of course, was the Creator–the Almighty God of whom they spoke, to whom they prayed, and about whom they studied daily in the Bible.

That should have been the end of it. And apparently it was at first. But *confusion*–neither of, nor from, God or the Bible–has seemed to reign supreme in the recovery "theology" from 1940 on. Long prior to his attaining sobriety in the Oxford Group and A.A., Bill had been an atheist–calling himself a "conservative atheist." (See Dick B., *New Light on Alcoholism; God, Sam Shoemaker*, and A.A. 2d ed. [Kihei, HI: Paradise Research Publications, 1999], p. 91.) His wife Lois belonged to a sect known as Swedenborgians–characterizing herself as a "non-Christian." (See *Lois Remembers* [NY: Al-Anon Family Group Headquarters, 1979], pp. 2, 26.) This certainly meant that neither was steeped in biblical Christian thinking. Furthermore, before he had met Dr. Bob in Akron, Bill had come under the heavy influence of the Oxford Group, of Rev. Sam Shoemaker, and of the thinking of long-dead Professor William James. This meant that these influences had offered to the non-religious Bill Wilson a nebulous "Power" to add to his mix.

This new "Power" which the doubting Wilson was later to embrace and "empower" did not gain ascendency in his life during his Bible study in the home of Dr. Bob and Anne Smith in the summer of 1935. In fact, as Dr. Bob's son "Smitty" was to write in the Foreword to one of my titles, "Before there was a Big Book–in the period of 'flying blind,' God's Big Book was the reference used in our home. The summer of 1935, when Bill lived with us, Dr. Bob had read the Bible completely three times. And the references that seemed consistent with the program goals were the Sermon on the Mount, 1 Corinthians 13, and the Book of James. At Anne's 'Quiet Time'–a daily period held with the alcoholics in our home, the Bible was used." (Dick B., *The Good Book and The Big Book: A.A.'s Roots in the Bible*, 2d ed. [Kihei, HI: Paradise Research Publications, 1997], p. ix.) Bill's "Power" was not even of great importance when Bill penned the manuscript that, as frequently revised, became the First Edition of his Big Book in the Spring of 1939. "God" was mentioned dozens of times in the First Edition. The "Power" was listed as a "higher power" twice; and even Bill still called that "power" God: "Its [the Big Book's] main object is to enable you to find a Power greater than yourself which will solve your problem . . . . And it means, of course, that we are going to talk about God. . . . even though it was impossible for any of us to fully define or comprehend that Power, which is God" (*Alcoholics Anonymous*, 4th ed., pp. 45-46).

Strange New "gods"

At this point in recovery program history, Bill's "power" has acquired confused, distorted, conflicting, incredible meanings. It has even become a new "god" or "deity." No less a knowledgeable A.A. old-timer and, at times an official A.A. historian, than Mel B. has made the statement: "AA members have always issued disclaimers when discussing God: Typical is, 'Our program is spiritual, not religious.' If pressed for what the program's actual definition of *spiritual* is, however, it is doubtful that many A.A. members could explain" (Mel B., *New Wine: The Spiritual Roots of the Twelve Step Miracle* [MN: Hazelden, 1991], pp. 4-5). While this statement completely ignores the Bible emphasis in early A.A.'s "program" (as it was reported by Frank Amos to John D. Rockefeller, Jr. in 1938), it does illustrate Mel's awareness of the confusion that was set in motion almost as soon as Wilson returned from Akron in the summer of 1935 and fell back into the arms of his Oxford Group friends in New York, the counsel of Rev. Sam Shoemaker at Calvary Church, and the bizarre "higher powers" mentioned in the writings of Professor William James. (See the discussion below of the James ideas.)

The difficulty is that the A.A. and the recovery world of the 1940's and thereafter were soon at work devising dozens of strange names for the new god and later developing new godless theologies to support the nonsense. While some of her assumptions, descriptions, context, and sources leave much to be desired, I think it helpful to quote the following from Dr. Cathy Burns's title:

> Again, it should be unmistakable that AA's "Higher Power" is definitely not the God of the Bible, but AA literature makes it even plainer that other gods are acceptable. One particular alcoholic couldn't accept the idea of a "Higher Power." This is his account of how his AA sponsor explained it to him: THEN HE ASKS ME IF I BELIEVE IN A POWER GREATER THAN MYSELF, WHETHER I CALL THAT POWER GOD, *ALLAH, CONFUCIUS,* PRIME CAUSE, DIVINE MIND, *OR ANY OTHER NAME.* I TOLD HIM THAT I believe in electricity and other forces of nature, but as for a God, if there is one, He has never done anything for me. . . . "Then all of your troubles are over," says the man and leaves the room (Cathy Burns, *Alcoholics Anonymous Unmasked*, p. 39; emphasis added).

Far too many A.A. critics just mix up their history, their dates, their sources, and their quotes. It is therefore unfair to judge *early* A.A. by their statements. It is, however, quite fair to note that critics and researchers alike have an abundance of absurd names and quotes from today's recovery writings to support their statements that the new "deity" includes just about any god or "not-god" or sacred something one might choose to select.

Strange New "Theologies"

What is far more surprising, however, is the new theology that "researchers" are now attributing to A.A. itself. Please note the following from *Research on Alcoholics Anonymous: Opportunities and Alternatives*, edited by Barbara S. McCrady and William R. Miller (NJ: Publications Division of Rutgers Center of Alcohol Studies, 1993):

> Flores (1988) argues that there are a number of common misconceptions regarding A.A. . . . . Among the most common of these misconceptions are the beliefs that: . . . *A.A. is a religious organization.* The term "God" is either used or referred to in five of the 12 steps. However, God is defined as a "higher power" and ostensibly, can be extracted from a religious context and taken to be natural forces other than deity. Flores (1988) points out that it is up to AA members to come to their own personal understanding of the meaning and significance of this higher power (pp. 359-60).

> Spirituality as a term is, however, used in a considerably broader sense than that discussed so far. Spirituality in this sense appears to be referring to people who are concerned with metaphysical issues as well as their own day-to-day lives. It need have no belief in God. . . . But what is this spirituality if it is entirely outside of a traditional religious focus, and does this spirituality relate to Alcoholics Anonymous' "Higher Power"? Casual conversation suggests that spirituality might mean being thoughtful or engaging in meditation or just a general concern for metaphysical issues. . . . Spirituality can have a clearer definition than those noted above. Berenson (1990) suggests that 'spirituality, as opposed to religion, connotes a direct, personal experience of the sacred unmediated by particular belief systems

prescribed by dogma or by hierarchical structures of priests, ministers, rabbis, or gurus' (p. 304).

A.A. Pioneers seem to have studied, repeated, and believed the following verse from the Bible that appeared in almost every piece of religious literature they read or mentioned:

> Jesus saith unto him, I am the way, the truth, and the life: no man cometh unto the Father, but by me (John 14:6).

See these few, out of many, examples of such literature they read: Samuel M. Shoemaker, *Confident Faith* (NY: Fleming H. Revell, 1932), p. 46; Philip Marshall Brown, *The Venture of Belief* (NY: Fleming H. Revell, 1935), p. 49; Stephen Foot, *Life Began Yesterday* (NY: Harper & Brothers, 1935), p. 87; Olive M. Jones, *Inspired Children* (NY: Harper & Brothers, 1933), p. 50; Norma Smith Holm, *The Runner's Bible*, p. 21; James Moore Hickson, *Heal the Sick* (London: Methuen & Co., 1925), p. 266; Oswald Chambers, *Studies in the Sermon on the Mount* (Great Britain: Oswald Chambers Publications, 1995), p.102; many issues of *The Upper Room*; and the many highly studied titles of Glenn Clark, E. Stanley Jones, and Harry Emerson Fosdick.

Our exploration in this chapter should therefore concern the question: How did "recovery" move from the "Way" to irreligious "spirituality" to absurd deities. And certainly the best answers will come from a look at the compromise *names* that became a part of A.A.'s history.

Some "Higher Power" Homework: What Is This New "god"?

My Own Early Experiences

In grammar school, I said the Pledge of Allegiance to our flag. It talked of "one nation under God." Then I got hold of some coins and bills. And they *all* said "In God we trust." I joined the Boy Scouts, and I pledged that I would do my best to do my duty to God and my country. And, in the Army and when I was admitted to law practice, I must have sworn to uphold, protect, and defend the Constitution–knowing that one of our founding documents talked about our being "endowed by our Creator" with certain rights.

I never had any trouble knowing Who God was. And is! Actually, until I came to A.A., I never really met anyone else who had that trouble. That's not to say I didn't know what an atheist is: He or she is someone who doesn't believe in God. I also acquired some knowledge about what an agnostic is: He or she is someone who just plain doesn't know whether or not there is a God. Finally, I was the attorney for several Humanist groups in the course of my legal work; and I learned they didn't think there was a God at all. I also learned that, despite the Humanists' non-belief, the the courts have specifically ruled and held they are a "religion" (just as the courts have now frequently ruled that A.A. itself is a "religion").

When I came to Alcoholics Anonymous, I attended thousands of meetings and participated in hundreds of Big Book studies, Step Studies, Conferences, Conventions, and Groups. And I was sufficiently sick that I didn't give much thought to the frequent mention of "higher power" in meetings where I was present. The "higher power" stuff was, for me, just a phantom ship passing a sick drunk in the night. True, in the Big Book's 3rd edition, "higher power" was mentioned–but only twice–in its basic text (on page 43 and page 100). In both cases, the usage was clearly in the context of "God." Bill said so on pages 45 and 46 as well as page 100. Besides, I was told, that when you get to the Third Step and are still talking about a lightbulb or a doorknob as your "higher power," you will be baffled with a Third Step that says you are to turn your will and your life over to the care of God–a God it says you understood. In fact, that most of us very definitely understand to one degree or another. I certainly understood that this loving God is not a lightbulb or a doorknob.

Then I began to listen to the persistent talk in the fellowship about "higher power." Then to do some reading in A.A.'s later publications about this "higher power." Bill Wilson wrote in *Twelve Steps and Twelve Traditions* that you could make the A.A. "group" your higher power. My treatment center facilitators told me your higher power could be "good orderly direction." Speakers sometimes said at meetings that "it" could be "group of drunks." Therapists said, "Fake it till you make it" and "Act as if." Fake what, I thought! "Act as if *what,*" I again thought! And the more I listened, the more absurd the higher powers became in the language of "recovery"–the higher powers were tables, bulldozers, radiators, goddesses, "somethings," "any god you want," "yourself as not-god," the Big Dipper, Santa Claus, and–on Friday Nights, at our Larkspur Beginner's Meeting–"it" was regularly called "Ralph." Honest! It was! Sadly, today you can find all of these gods, not-gods, idols, and "somethings" in A.A.'s own "Conference Approved" literature and in many "scholarly" writings about the recovery field today. You can find the weird names and descriptions specifically documented in many of my books, particularly *The Oxford Group and Alcoholics Anonymous* (http://www.dickb.com/Oxford.shtml) and *The Good Book and The Big Book* (http://www.dickb.com/goodbook.shtml).

But if your life depended upon help from such a "higher power," wouldn't you want to know what that "higher power" was! I did. So I've been searching for 11 years not only to find out where A.A. came from, particularly in the Bible, but also how in the world someone threw Ralph into the mix. The longer I remained sober, the more ridiculous the Ralphs and the radiators seemed. Yet, in a telephone interview several years back, Bill Wilson's own secretary told me on the telephone that a higher power could be a chair. Of course, she was a Buddhist; and perhaps, in her thinking, there might be a god in a chair. But such a god has no reputation for curing drunks. I sure know it isn't the Creator or "God"–the God that Bill Wilson often called "Our Father" and Dr. Bob called my "Heavenly Father," as did Jesus Christ, God's only begotten Son.

Let's Start with the Bible to Look for a "higher power"

Dr. Bob said many times that A.A.'s basic ideas came from the Bible. You can find that in *DR. BOB and the Good Oldtimers* and in Dr. Bob's last major address in Detroit in 1948. You can see it in his talks and in the pamphlets he commissioned in Akron. To this day, I've never found or heard anything that indicates Bill Wilson disputed Dr. Bob's statement about the Bible's being the source of A.A.'s basic ideas. Nor could he. Because, even if A.A. had been borrowed exclusively from the teachings of Reverend Sam Shoemaker or exclusively from the Oxford Group itself (and it wasn't), neither of those sources propounded any idea about Almighty God's being called some idol like Ralph, a radiator, or a table. Or "Gertrude"–another god I recently found in one particular scholar's early, anonymous work.

Does the Bible Speak of a "higher power?" What does the Bible say a "higher power" is? My research in *Young's Analytical Concordance*, in the Bible itself, and in several Bible dictionaries shows no reference to "God" as a "higher power." There is a reference in Romans to "higher powers;" but the reference quite clearly is not to the Creator–saying, instead, there is *no* power but of God:

> Rom. 13:1,2:
> Let every soul be subject unto the higher powers. For there is no power but of God: the powers that be are ordained of God.
> Whosoever therefore resisteth the power, resisteth the ordinance of God: and they that resist shall receive to themselves damnation.

The Good Book Commands: "Thou shalt have no other gods before me [i.e., Yahweh]". There are plenty of references to the Creator, Yahweh, as the "high" or "highest" God, but God makes it clear that there are to be no other gods before Him–nowhere! Not in chairs. Not in light bulbs. Not in radiators. Not in yourself. Not even in Alcoholics Anonymous:

Exodus 20:3-5:
Thou shalt have no other gods before me
Thou shalt not make unto thee any graven image, or any likeness *of any thing* that *is* in heaven above, or that *is* in the earth beneath, or that *is* in the water under the earth.
Thou shalt not bow down thyself to them, nor serve them. . . .

There *is* One with all power: The Creator, Yahweh, the Highest, the God of power.

- **He Is High All Right**

  Psalm 99:2:
  The Lord *is* great in Zion; and he *is* high above the people.

  Genesis 14:20:
  And blessed be the most high God, which hath delivered thine enemies into thy hand. . . .

  Psalm 93:4:
  The Lord on high *is* mightier than the noise of many waters, yea, *than* the mighty waves of the sea.

  Psalm 78:35:
  And they remembered that God *was* their rock, and the high God their redeemer.

- **The Most High**

  Psalm 92:8:
  But thou, Lord, *art most* high for evermore.

  Daniel 5:18:
  O thou king, the most high God gave Nebuchadnezzar thy father a kingdom, and majesty, and glory, and honour.

Mark 5:7:
And cried with a loud voice, and said, What have I to do
with thee, Jesus, *thou* Son of the most high God?

•   **In Truth, the Highest**

Luke 6:35,36:
But love ye your enemies, and do good, and lend, hoping for
nothing again; and your reward shall be great, and ye shall
be the children of the Highest: for he is kind unto the
unthankful and *to* the evil.
Be *ye* therefore merciful, as your Father also is merciful.

The Good Book Says of the Creator: For *Thine* Is the Power

Psalm 145:11,12:
They shall speak of the glory of thy kingdom and talk of thy
power.
To make known to the sons of men his mighty acts, and the
glorious majesty of his kingdom.

Psalm 147:5:
Great *is* our Lord, and of great power: his understanding *is*
infinite.

Psalm 150:1,2:
Praise ye the Lord. Praise God in his sanctuary: praise him
in the firmament of his power.
Praise him for his mighty acts: praise him according to his
excellent greatness.

Matthew 6:10, 13:
Thy kingdom come. Thy will be done in earth, as *it is* in heaven.
And lead us not into temptation, but deliver us from evil:
For thine is the kingdom, and the power, and the glory, for
ever. Amen.

Ephesians 6:10, 11:
Finally, my brethren, be strong in the Lord, and in the power
of his might.
Put on the whole armour of God, that ye may be able to
stand against the wiles of the devil.

1 Corinthians 2:4, 5:
And my speech and my preaching was not with enticing
words of man's wisdom, but in demonstration of the Spirit
and of power;
That your faith should not stand in the wisdom of men, but
in the power of God.

And the Bible Has Much More: For a much more thorough and
complete study, in the Bible itself, of God's name, nature, will,
power, commandments, and so on, see my titles: *By the Power of God*
(http://www.dickb.com/powerofgod.shtml) and *Why Early A.A.
Succeeded* (http://www.dickb.com/aabiblestudy.shtml).

Bill Wilson, Dr. Bob Smith, and the Other Pioneers
Spoke in the Beginning Only of the Creator

I've spent 11 years endeavoring to learn if A.A. was based on the
Bible. It was clear, when I began, that Dr. Bob said so. It was clear
that Bill W. seems never to have disputed the statement. And the
Frank Amos report to John D. Rockefeller, Jr., spoke only of the
Bible in reporting on early A.A. and its "Program."

When you read the Big Book's repeated references to "Creator" with
a capital "C," to "Maker" with a capital "M," to "Father" with a
capital "F," and to all its other Bible descriptions and mention of
Almighty God, you will have a hard time finding a light bulb, a
radiator, or a group that's called our living God. The idols,
"somethings," "not-gods," and chairs came later. But compromise
description of, and claims for, the status of a "god" are as old as the
Bible itself. The Creator, God Almighty, Yahweh, doesn't speak

kindly of our having anything to do with other names, other gods, or any other phoney "powers."

There is no need for any of us to think someone is trying to foist Christianity or the Bible or even God Himself on present-day A.A. It can't be done. Not the way things are now. But it violates no Traditions, no principles, and no Steps of A.A. to let people in on our history and on the early A.A. reliance on the Creator. For our Pioneers always confirmed the source of early A.A.'s "miracle"—the Creator.

It really may cost A.A. something in the sale of its reams of literature if people return to discussing and pinpointing the history of God in A.A.. After all, you can read a Gideon Bible for free in most hotel rooms. Such discussion of God may *and does* bother some people who don't believe in God or the Bible. It may *and does* cause some treatment centers or therapists to think people won't check in if there is mention of Almighty God or of A.A.'s religious roots. But it does no service to anyone to put a lid on God.

As I've said so often: AAs may be sick when they walk into the rooms of A.A., but they are not stupid. Many A.A. old-timers say to this very day: "If the word "God" scares you out of these rooms, a bottle of booze will scare you back. . . . if you live that long" (See as to one source of this expression: Dick B. *That Amazing Grace: The Role of Clarence and Grace S. in Alcoholics Anonymous* [Kihei, HI: Paradise Research Publications, 1996], p. 89).

Sure, people stop drinking without God. Certainly, people get sober without A.A. In fact, people get sober *in* A.A. while "relying" upon some phantom "higher power." In so doing, all these people–probably without even knowing it–have directly or indirectly added something to A.A. that's not the original, genuine coin of the realm. For, as Bill Wilson said:

Belief in the power of God, plus enough willingness, honesty and humility to establish and maintain the new order of things, were the essential requirements (*Alcoholics Anonymous*, 4th ed., pp. 13-14).

Despite all we can say, many who are real alcoholics are not going to believe they are in that class. By every form of self-deception and experimentation, they will try to prove themselves exceptions to the rule, therefore nonalcoholic. If anyone who is showing inability to control his drinking can do the right-about-face and drink like a gentleman, our hats are off to him. Heaven knows, we have tried hard enough and long enough to drink like other people (*Alcoholics Anonymous*, 4th ed., p. 31).

We trust infinite God rather than our finite selves. . . . We never apologize to anyone for depending upon our Creator (*Alcoholics Anonymous*, 4th ed., p. 68).

If he [the candidate for A.A.] thinks he can do the job in some other way, or prefers some other spiritual approach, encourage him to follow his own conscience. We have no monopoly on God; we merely have an approach that worked with us (*Alcoholics Anonymous*, 4th ed., p. 95).

Typically, Dr. Bob said it much more simply:

If you think you are an atheist, an agnostic, a skeptic, or have any other form of intellectual pride which keeps you from accepting what is in this book, I feel sorry for you. . . . Your Heavenly Father will never let you down! (*Alcoholics Anonymous*, 4th ed., p. 181).

Here's Your "higher power" Homework

Origin Unknown. I don't know where Bill Wilson got his "higher power." As far as I can ascertain, he never told us. He definitely dabbled in spiritualism. He definitely dabbled in "New Thought." He definitely dabbled in the writings of Williams James.

There are even at least two Oxford Group writings that mention a "higher power" (though Oxford Group activist and expert Rev. T. Willard Hunter told me personally that he had never heard in the Oxford Group of any "higher power"). So, like today's mysterious "Bin Laden," our "higher power"–varying in location and scope and description from a chair to Santa Claus–seems to be hiding its roots. If you find those roots, please let us all know. I have a hunch you will find the "higher power" is really God in the minds of those who use the phrase. But they are scared to death to surrender and admit their need for God. Or they are scared to death of a church or their former church. Or they just plain don't want to read the Bible, or our history, or perhaps not even the Big Book and its earlier manuscripts (Compare the facts in: *Turning Point: A History of Early A.A.'s Spiritual Roots and Successes*. http://www.dickb.com/Turning.shtml).

Some Sources Which Were Probably Read by Some Early AAs–Sources Which *You* Can Research. Some Pioneer AAs did read the following titles which mention a "higher power" of one sort or another: (1) Ralph Waldo Trine, *In Tune with the Infinite: Or Fullness of Peace, Power, and Plenty* (NY: Thomas H. Crowell, 1897); (2) William James, *The Varieties of Religious Experience* (NY: First Vintage Press/The Library of America Edition, 1990); (3) Elwood Worcester, Samuel McComb, and Isador H. Coriat, *Religion and Medicine: The Moral Control of Nervous Disorders* (NY: Moffat, Yard & Company, 1908); (4) Victor C. Kitchen, *I Was a Pagan* (NY: Harper & Brothers, 1934); (5) A. J. Russell, *For Sinners Only* (London: Hodder & Stoughton, 1932). And are there more? I'm inclined to think there may be because of the large numbers of new thought writers of that era, the immense research and writing done by William James, the interest in "mind-cure" ideas, and the popularity of Victor Kitchen with Bill Wilson and in the New York Oxford Group circles.

I personally have no particular interest in "new thought" literature. Nor am I a fan of the religious views, whatever they may be, of William James, the psychologist. Nor has much evidence come to my attention concerning even the possible successes of McComb, et al. Nor do I find anything in Kitchen's writing that suggests he was simply referring to some "Higher Power," with which he needed to establish a relationship, but which he came to recognize as God as a result of his Oxford Group experiences. Nor, however, have I seen much in any of the foregoing writings (other than Kitchen's) that suggests a strong belief in the power of the Creator; or in the necessity for coming to Him through confessing Jesus as Lord and believing God raised Jesus from the dead (Romans 10:9). My particular interest, as is known by many, is in the Bible; the truth about God, His power, and His will that can be found in the Bible; the necessity for coming to Him through Jesus Christ (Romans 10:9); and the exceedingly abundant power and healing available to those of us who choose that route (see Ephesians 3:20). In fact, I have found that even Bill Wilson's medical mentor, Dr. William Duncan Silkworth, had spoken positively about making the turn to Jesus Christ (whom Silkworth and Wilson both called the Great Physician) for the healing of alcoholism (see *The Positive Power of Jesus Christ* by Norman Vincent Peale).

This next part may prove helpful to you in tracking the origin and meaning of "higher power" and help you do more research on that subject if you care to. It's sure not my area of expertise.

Some Additional "Higher Power" Homework: Where Did This New "god" Come from?

No Need for a Label

In the previous part, I hope we established that we (or at least I) don't know what this new "god" is. We don't know what a "higher power" is. AAs have called "it" a something, a not-god, an "any god," a "group," and Gertrude. You know all the other names–lightbulb, radiator, and so on. So it doesn't seem necessary to put a label on this "higher power" phenomenon. "It" can be just about anything! We don't necessarily need to put it in a box and call it "higher-power-ism" either. Nor is "it" just an A.A. higher-power-ism. You can find it in most 12 Step Groups, in self-help groups, in "anonymous" groups, and even in many Christian recovery groups. But you sure can't find it in the Bible.

Whence Came "higher-power-ism?"

I'll tell you at the outset that I don't know. I do know it didn't come from the Bible, and we've already covered that. Moreover, Bill Wilson said that no one "invented" A.A. So–true or false–Bill's statement indicates he wasn't taking credit for "it" or for any other specific ideas in A.A.'s spiritual program of recovery–even the ones that came from the Bible. Despite these truths, you find scholarly writers laying a laudatory trip on Alcoholics Anonymous and its very special "higher power." For example, Walter Houston Clark, Professor of the Psychology of Religion, had these things to say:

> . . . Preach faith till you have it and then, because you have it, you will preach faith." When a neophyte applies to Alcoholics Anonymous and is told he must rely on a Power greater than himself for strength, he often objects that he believes in no Higher Power. The reply is that he must behave as if there were a Higher Power. This frequently results in what is in effect a true conversion in which, whether by slow process or swift, atheists and agnostics often arrive at a belief in God (Walter Houston Clark. *The Psychology of Religion: An Introduction to Religious Experience and Behavior* [New York: MacMillan, 1958], pp. 195-96).

Professor Clark demonstrates his lack of knowledge of A.A. and helps compound the questionable and erroneous later language and theories that were added to A.A.'s "spiritual" precepts. You'd think–from the foregoing remarks–that Professor Clark was describing some religion. First, he quoted the itinerant Methodist preacher, John Wesley, on preaching faith. Then Clark says a neophyte "applies" to A.A.–which he doesn't. And can't. A neophyte (otherwise known as a drunk) just plain shows up unless some court or treatment center orders or takes him to a meeting. Then, says Clark, the newcomer "must rely on a Power greater than himself." Must? The Big Book says that A.A. spirituality means dependence upon our **Creator**! (Alcoholics Anonymous 4th ed., p. 68). With just such fallacious reasoning as that of Clark, the compromise process begins–similar, in a way, to the deception of Eve in the Garden of Eden. Add a word. Subtract a word. Change a word. And soon, no word. Clark must also be faulted for tendering an easily repudiated canard; he claims without qualification: The newcomer says "he believes in no Higher Power." But I have never heard that language used, in the Big Book or in meetings. A newcomer occasionally says he is an atheist or that he doesn't believe in God. However, I've yet to hear one even mention, let alone deny belief in some "higher power." You have to come into A.A.'s influence to get hit with a "higher power. And, regrettably, the newcomer is seldom turned away these days from his "higher power" if and when he "gets" one.

And what "higher power"? How did that forbidden fruit get planted in *our A.A.* Garden? I've yet to speak to an un-indoctrinated newcomer who didn't say that he *believed* in God! It's how you pose the question that produces the result. Next, Clark introduces the William James "act as if" language. This despite the fact that probably no newcomer but Bill Wilson, and probably Dr. Bob, ever read William James in early sobriety or even thereafter. Try reading it. It's a bear! And Professor Clark then just plain ignores everything in the Bible from Romans 10:9 to John 3:1-16. Clark asserts that this higher-power-ism "process" frequently results in a "true" conversion. No Bible verses. No documentation. No apparent understanding of, or definition of, "conversion." No mention of Jesus. And no support in the Big Book. In fact, the most you might say today is that most atheists and agnostics would–if they actually did what Clark says they do–wind up with a belief in a radiator. And *retain* that bizarre idea. In fact, preach it. I hear that idea on the rare occasions when an e-mail from an atheist or agnostic really does tell me about god.

I have no particular mission to single out or attack Dr. Clark's position. He's actually surrounded by a hundred modern writings that tell you how to find anything but God in A.A. through a mystical process that doesn't involve Jesus Christ or the Bible or the receipt of the gift of the Holy Spirit. This new "god" of the revisionist writers just "growed"! It keeps growing too–in diversity and seeming importance. If you would like to have the names and writings of people who have promoted the new, humanist/revisionist "god" of recovery, just read the bibliographies in those of my books which list "A.A. Pro and Con;" i.e., http://www.dickb.com/titles.shtml.

Now for Your Additional Homework

As I've said, I don't know where "higher power" came from. I do know it didn't come from God or from the Good Book. Here, however, are some of the sources a few AAs were exposed to and which perhaps triggered the new "ism":

Ralph Waldo Trine:

Said the great Hindu sage, Manu, He who in his own soul perceives the Supreme Soul in all beings, and acquires equanimity toward them all, attains the highest bliss. It was Athanasius who said, Even we may become Gods walking about in the flesh. The same great truth we are considering is the one that runs through the life and teachings of Gautama, he who became the Buddha. People are in bondage, said he, because they have not yet removed the idea of I. To do away with all sense of separateness, and to recognize the oneness of the self with the Infinite, is the spirit that breathes through all his teachings. Running through the lives of all the mediaeval mystics was this same great truth. Then, coming near our own time, we find the highly illumined seer, Emanuel Swedenborg. . . . All through the world's history we find that the men and women who have entered into the realm of true wisdom and power, and hence into the realm of true peace and joy, have lived in harmony with this **Higher Power** (Ralph Waldo Trine, *In Tune with the Infinite: Or*

Fullness of Peace Power and Plenty. 1933 ed. [Indianapolis: Bobbs-Merrill, 1897], pp 198-99; bold face added).

Trine talks of the Hindu, the teachings of Buddha, the mystics, and the spiritualist Emanuel Swedenborg (of whom Lois Wilson was a follower). But nary a mention of the Bible or of Yahweh, the Creator in the foregoing "Higher Power" dissertation. The writings of Trine and other "New Thought" authors were studied by some early AAs, including Dr. Bob. In fact, the Emmet Fox books are still frequently mentioned in A.A.

William James:

If there be **higher powers** able to impress us, they may get access to us only through the subliminal door (William James, *The Varieties of Religious Experience* [New York: First Vintage Books/The Library of America Edition, 1990], p. 224; bold face added).

The solution is a sense that we are saved from the wrongness by making proper connection with the **higher powers** (James, *The Varieties of Religious Experience*, p. 442; bold face added).

The whole array of Christian saints and heresiarchs, including the greatest, the Bernards, the Loyolas, the Luthers, the Foxes, the Wesleys, had their visions, voices, rapt conditions, guiding impressions, and 'openings.'. . . The subjects here actually feel themselves played upon by powers beyond their will. The evidence is dynamic: the God or spirit moves the very organs of their body. The great field for this sense of being the instrument of a **higher power** is of course 'inspiration' (James, *The Varieties of Religious Experience*, p. 428-29; bold face added).

The difficulty with Professor William James is that he lumps his "higher powers" and "higher power" into one bin–a receptacle which includes discussions of inspiration, being an instrument, receiving openings, and access by subliminal doors. And, in discussing experiences with these phenomena, James further pumps hypnotism, "suggestion," "diabolical possession," "hystero-demonopathy," "prophecy," and "levitation" into his wide-ranging analysis. It is safe to say, I believe, that William James was not confining his discussion of "higher power" to Yahweh, the Creator.

The result of the William James influence on Sam Shoemaker and on Bill Wilson, for me, seems to require my having to listen–one hundred years later–to AAs both in California and in Hawaii talking about a "higher power," "spiritualism," "spirituality," the Eleventh Step, and "sexual fantasies" all in one breath. And they most assuredly do, which is precisely what I believe can happen when you "open" your mind to the intrusion of compromise and spiritual wickedness into a Bible-based recovery program. And, to quote Lois Wilson, apparently in pursuit of a "universal spiritual program" (*Lois Remembers: Memoirs of the co-founder of Al-Anon and wife of the co-founder of Alcoholics Anonymous* [NY: Al-Anon Family Group Headquarters, 1979], p. 113).Would that the Wilsons–either or both–had heeded Bill's favorite Book of James in the Bible. For James 4:7 states: "Submit yourselves therefore to God. Resist the devil, and he will flee from you." I believe the early influences of Professor James on A.A. were definitely corrupting. They did not seem to produce any resistence whatever to their devilish nature and impact. Again, quoting the Book of James: "This wisdom descendeth not from above, but *is* earthly, sensual, devilish" (James 3:16). Even today, one website moderator who specifically excludes all such writing, including mine, from her A.A. "history" game preserve calls the making of the foregoing remarks "preaching." I call them quoting! AAs read the *Book* of James far more than they read *William* James. They so favored the Book of James that they even wanted to call their new Fellowship *The James Club*–and they weren't referring to the good professor.

The more AAs have listened to the revisionists in the last fifty years, the farther the program has moved from the Bible to its present "any god," "not-god," and "something" idol worship. One of the many new gods appearing in revisionist literature is that the "higher power" is simply that which gets you sober. Disulfiram (Antabuse)? Naltrexone (ReVia)? Acupuncture? Hypnosis? Therapy? Forced attendance? Meetings? Service? A "group" of drunks? A lightbulb? (And see Clarence Snyder. *My Higher Power the Lightbulb* [Florida: Steve Foreman, 1982]). One new writer on the scene says this:

> Belief in something transcendental–a "higher power," outside of the individual–is part of the program, and prayer and meditation are seen as the principal means of conscious contact with this "higher power." The idea is not so much to pray to God for help in finding a way out of an alcohol problem; it has more to do with *humility*–"cleaning house" so that the "grace of God can enter us and expel the obsession." . . . . AAs Twelve Steps and Twelve Traditions stresses that AA does not demand belief in anything" (Anne M. Fletcher. *Sober for Good* [Boston: Houghton Mifflin, 2001], pp. 240-41).

My, oh my! Whatever happened to Dr. Bob's assurance that "Your Heavenly Father will never let you down!"

Elwood Worcester, Samuel McComb, and Isador H. Coriat

> Now among the things which seem to tell against faith in the infinite goodness of the Power which this universe discloses are the facts of pain and disease. . . . But if the order of nature is the expression of the Divine Will it follows that God wills health, that He means his creatures to be healthy, and that He is opposed to pain, disease, abnormality of every kind, just as He is opposed to sin and vice (Elwood Worcester, Samuel McComb, and Isador H. Coriat, *Religion and Medicine: The Moral Control of Nervous Disorders* [New York: Moffat, Yard & Company, 1908], p. 292).

> However man first became aware of a Spirit behind or within this universe, he has been aware of it, and he has felt that in this Infinite Spirit he lives and that on this Spirit his life and salvation depend. Not only has man been conscious of his dependence on a **higher Power**, but also he has sought to bring himself more

and more into harmonious relations with this Power, and his desire goes forth in prayer. In a sense prayer is man's language with God (Worcester, etc., *Religion and Medicine*, p. 304; bold face added).

A diligent, researching, AA, named Cliff M., called the *Religion and Medicine* citation to my attention, for which I thank him. The three *Religion and Medicine* authors rejected Christian Science and other New Thought ideas and quoted much from the Bible to support the idea that God is and has the "Power" to heal man and keep him healthy. For them and probably for the Emmanuel Movement of which they wrote, God was the "higher" "Power" upon which they sought to rely for treatment. And that is the concept that Bill Wilson spelled out on pages 43, 45, and 46 of the Fourth Edition and earlier editions of the Big Book when Bill spoke of a "Higher Power," said he was going to talk about "God," and then defined the "Power" *as* "God." Quite a difference from his writing in *Twelve Steps and Twelve Traditions* where readers were invited to consider the option that this "higher power" could be the "group." That particular nonsense sent me spinning for months in an A.A. Step Meeting until my mind really began to heal and clear. Yet it has become doctrinal these days in many a meeting room.

Victor C. Kitchen

The re-direction of old desires and substitution for old stimuli has extended not only throughout my sensual life, but into my social and intellectual life as well. It enters into all of my thinking and into all of my dealings with other people. When, for instance, I only *thought* about God—when He existed only in my mind as a belief—I could reach Him only as an intellectual conclusion. I concluded that there must be some **Higher Power** to account for all the things taking place in space much as scientists concluded that there must be an atom to account for all the things taking place in physics (Victor C. Kitchen, *I Was a Pagan* [New York: Harper & Brothers, 1934], p. 85; bold face added).

Victor Kitchen was a good friend of Bill Wilson's. Kitchen was a member of the same Oxford Group businessman's team of which Bill was a member around 1935-1936. Kitchen wrote articles for Rev. Sam Shoemaker's *Calvary Evangel.* He was a member of the Oxford Group team that brought the Oxford Group to the famous Firestone events of the 1933 period–events that led to the recovery of Dr. Bob in Akron. Kitchen's *I Was a Pagan* was a very popular book about the time Bill Wilson was getting sober. It uses many phrases similar to those of Wilson. (See Dick B., *The Oxford Group and Alcoholics Anonymous* [http://www.dickb.com/Oxford.shtml]).

If you want to know whether Kitchen thought his "Higher Power" was Almighty God and that you came to him through His Son Jesus Christ, just read *I Was a Pagan.* In two words. *Kitchen did.* He tells how he stopped pursuing false gods (as he called them) and came to believe in the one, true living God as God is described in the Bible.

Canon L. W. Grenstead. The most popular title written by **A. J. Russell** was *For Sinners Only: The Book of the Oxford Groups* (New York: Harper & Brothers Publishers, 1932). My good friend and Oxford Group authority Reverend T. Willard Hunter told me some years back that he had never heard "Higher Power" used in the Oxford Groups. However, we've seen above that Victor Kitchen used it, albeit in the context of Almighty God. And I've found that, if you keep looking long enough, the influence of compromise language and universalism in the Oxford Group, as well as the ideas of William James, seem to have pushed "Higher Power" into the Oxford Group niche from time to time. Thus, Russell has a chapter of his title devoted to an interview with Canon L. W. Grenstead, "one of the foremost scholars and psychologists in the Church of England, Oriel Professor of the Philosophy of the Christian Religion, the Bampton Lecturer of 1930, a member of the Archbishop's Committee on Doctrine and on Spiritual Healing, and Canon of Liverpool" (p. 236). Russell quotes Canon Grenstead as follows:

> The Group [Oxford Group] change men. They know that if you
> try to solve a conflict by effort from within, you never solve it.
> But if you try to solve it by a higher Power from without you
> always solve it, though the solution may not necessarily be what
> you or others expect (pp. 239-40).

The next few pages include the Canon's remarks on "Guidance. . . the
work of the Holy Spirit in human life" and "willingness to do the Will
of God . . . the measure of a man's true understanding of His will"
(pp. 241-42); and such remarks leave little doubt in my mind that
Grenstead was consistently speaking of the Creator as *the* "higher
Power."

Norman Vincent Peale. During my hour-long interview and
visit in Pawling, New York, with Dr. Norman Vincent Peale, that
famous preacher and religious leader stated to me that he had never
met anyone who didn't think that God was the "Higher Power" to
which Bill Wilson referred. Peale was a long-time friend of Wilson's
and a long-time supporter of A.A. Later, I found Peale had written the
following in his best-selling book:

> For many years I have been interested in the problem of the
> alcoholic and in the organization known as Alcoholics
> Anonymous. One of their basic principles is that before a person
> can be helped he must recognize that he is an alcoholic and that
> of himself he can do nothing; that he has no power within
> himself; that he is defeated. When he accepts this point of view
> he is in a position to receive help from other alcoholics and from
> the **Higher Power–God** (Norman Vincent Peale, *The Power of
> Positive Thinking* [New York: Prentice-Hall, Inc., 1952], p. 230;
> bold face added).

In the same book, Peale related the story of a man who had said he
had no interest in religion, who was fighting a losing battle over
alcoholism, and was persuaded to attend an Alcoholics Anonymous
meeting. The alcoholic said that a rebirth had taken place. He went to

church. Peale told of his friendship with the man and of the man's telling him (Peale) this:

> Just where my new life began is a matter that is difficult to determine. Whether it was when I met Carl in the bar [who had suggested A.A.], or wrestling past the drinking places [asking God to help him get past the places], or at the Alcoholics Anonymous meeting, or at the church, I do not know. But I, who had been a hopeless alcoholic for twenty-five years, suddenly became a sober man. I could never have done this alone, for I had tried it a thousand times and failed. **But I drew upon a Higher Power and the Higher Power, which is God, did it** (Peale, *The Power of Positive Thinking*, p. 233; bold face added).

The date Carl's new life began was April 24, 1947. To paraphrase the Archie Bunker theme song: Those were the days! Dr. Bob was still alive. The first edition of the Big Book–published in 1939–was still the basic text. Wilson had not yet written his own treatises (*Alcoholics Anonymous Comes of Age* and *Twelve Steps and Twelve Traditions*). The "Higher Power" of those days was God! In the words of a well-known comedian, "Let's have a little respect, please!" What a boon it would to the dismal recovery scene of today if all the government agencies, grant-subsidized research projects, and other scholars, historians, revisionists, therapists, and treatment people would take a look at the real A.A. of yesteryear, as seen by those who were there: Fosdick, Peale, Shoemaker, Buchman, Lupton, Russell, Hazard, Cornell, and even Bill's beloved, but drunken Ebby (Bill's sponsor). They all talked about God! Just God! Only God!

And that completes your homework assignment which has been covered in two foregoing two parts that ask "who is this new god" and "whence came this new god."–the One that has become a lightbulb, just any old idol, a "something," and even nothing at all. The One which our Big Book nonetheless says is our Creator and has all power!

What Is "a Power greater than ourselves"?
Another New "god" in A.A.? Or the Creator?

An Early A.A. Experience I'd Like to Share

Let me introduce you to Rich. He's a young newcomer I met at my
Wednesday night Home Meeting more than ten years ago. A friend
of mine named John came up to me, pointed to Rich (who was sitting
alone), and asked me to talk to him. I asked why. John replied:
Because he came out of the same treatment center I did. He's fresh
out. And I know you like to work with newcomers. So approach Rich
I did. He was about twenty-one years old, had a job, had just gotten
out of treatment, and was following their instructions to "go to a
meeting."

After the meeting, I asked Rich to come to my apartment where we
could talk more about A.A. He did; and, after some general questions
and comments, I asked him if he believed in God.

Rich's immediate comment was: "They told me it could be a tree."
And I'd heard that one before.

I asked Rich to step over to the big window in my apartment. The
window looked out on a beautiful forest of Redwoods, Oaks, Bays,
and other indigenous trees. I said: Rich. Look out there. What do you
see? He replied: Trees. I asked: Do you think any one or all of those
trees created the heavens and the earth? He said: I get your point. And
that was the last I heard of trees from Rich. In fact, he's been sober
for many years now. He's over 30, married, has a great job, and has
a youngster on the way. I'm hoping he will name the child "Richard."
The problem is that, if he does, it could be named after Rich or
myself. Either way, I'll probably claim the credit.

Rich has gone to thousands of meetings, just as I have. He's been a
speaker at, and secretary of, many A.A. meetings. He's been to A.A.

Conferences, to Big Book Seminars, and to lots of fun events like A.A. dances, camp-outs, and visits to comedy shows. I was his A.A. sponsor for several years and took him through the Twelve Steps. In turn, he's sponsored many men in their recovery and taken them through the Twelve Steps. He took Bible classes, became a born again Christian, and attended our Bible fellowship. His aunt is a Roman Catholic Nun. His sister is married to a Jew. I've never heard him criticize either religious denomination. I guess he has had good exposure to several now because his wife is also a Christian. But I've never heard him talk about a tree.

In fact, a few years ago, Rich was coming to Hawaii to get married at a beautiful site on the North Shore of Oahu. He phoned and asked me to be his Best Man. We went to the wedding site, which was surrounded by flowers, rocks, a creek, a beautiful waterfall. And trees. But I never heard either Rich or the officiating minister say a word about a tree–even during the prayers. And, since I keep in touch with him, I can say that I've never heard Rich talk about trees as God since that long ago day in my apartment. But when I ask him: Who loves you? He still answers: God does, and you do, Dick. And we do.

A Brief Look at What the Wilson "Power" Was in Early A.A.

Prior to publication of the First Edition of the Big Book in 1939, Bill Wilson prepared a number of draft manuscripts. In what purports to be the very first draft of the Second Step, here's an alleged statement of what Bill then wrote:

> [Allegedly in the "very first draft of the Twelve Steps. . . This is an approximate reconstruction of the way he first set them down" (quoting the original draft of Steps 2 and 3)]: "2. Came to believe that God could restore us to sanity. 3. Made a decision to turn our wills and our lives over to the care and direction of God" (*Pass It On: The Story of Bill Wilson and how the A.A. message reached the world* [New York: Alcoholics Anonymous World Services, 1984], p. 198).

Dr. Bob died. Wilson decided to write his own essays and his own history. And these were edited with a fine tooth comb by two Jesuit priests, Father John C. Ford and Father Ed Dowling. Bill inserted his new idea: "You can, if you wish, make A.A. itself your 'higher power'" (*Twelve Steps and Twelve Traditions* [New York: Alcoholics Anonymous World Services, p. 27]).

Then, in his version of A.A. history, Bill added his own, expanded version of the change he had wrought in substituting "Power" for "God" in the Second Step:

> In Step Two we decided to describe God as a Power greater than ourselves. . . . Such were the final concessions to those of little or no faith; this was the great contribution of our atheists and agnostics. They had widened the gateway so that all who suffer might pass through, regardless of their belief *or lack of belief.* God was certainly there in our Steps, but He was now expressed in terms that anybody–*anybody at all*–could accept and try" (*Alcoholics Anonymous Comes of Age* [New York: Alcoholics Anonymous World Services, 1957], p. 167; italics in the original).

There may be lots more history about what, and why Bill did what he did, with his new "group-Power" substitution for God. But the foregoing will suffice in light of our two previous sections on "higher power" and our next section to come, discussing "God as we understood Him." The simple fact is, that under pressure from a couple of atheists–perhaps only one supposed atheist (Hank Parkhurst)–Bill had boldly reversed the original A.A. idea of a conversion, with restoration to sanity, and a cure by God Almighty.

For illustrations of the original Pioneer attitude, see how it is still expressed in *Alcoholics Anonymous,* 4th ed:

> God had restored his sanity (p. 57).
> Your Heavenly Father will never let you down! (p. 181).

Henrietta, the Lord has been so wonderful to me, curing me of this terrible disease, that I just want to keep talking about it and telling people (p. 191).

Had Bill Wilson evicted the Creator from the rooms of Alcoholics Anonymous subsequent to 1939? From my standpoint, of course, that was and is impossible. Still, was A.A. no longer a place for restoration to sanity by God? For a cure of alcoholism by the Lord? Had the A.A. rooms been opened to "somethings," "not gods," "any gods," a "group power," or a "somebody else" as restorative, healing forces?

Not if you could receive or had received the restoration, healing, and deliverance that Dr. Bob said that he did. That Bill Wilson *said* he did. That the pioneers did. That I did. For–just like those Pioneers–I had relied upon the Creator, and here I am today. He didn't let me down. But what of this "Power greater than ourselves" that has turned so many 12 Step people toward light bulbs, chairs, groups, radiators, and Ralph. Quite frankly, I don't know. Bill Wilson is dead, and he can't tell us. Yet many of his successors at the helm of A.A.'s publishing arm appear to think you can be healed by a lightbulb or a radiator or the other idols. Thankfully, however, there is still plenty of room for some homework–research that will enable a full, frank, and accurate comparison of these revisionist interpretations of the "Power greater than ourselves" phrase with some of the very clear original Big Book language about "that Power, which is God." (See, for example, *Alcoholics Anonymous*, 4the ed., p. 46.) Then *you–who are seeking recovery inside or outside of Twelve Step Fellowships*–can choose the radiator or the living God for your power in recovery. And do so with knowledge that the radiator didn't come from God or the Bible or early A.A.

Revisionist Ideas about "Power-greater-than-ourselves-ism"

The Unabridged Version of Early AAs. A.A. worked! Forty pioneers–real alcoholics all–had recovered from their medically incurable malady of alcoholism. They had used no Steps because there were no Steps. Their parent group–the Oxford Group–had helped alcoholics with no steps, no "six" steps, and certainly no Twelve Steps. In the words of A.A.'s own literature:

> They [the forty pioneers] had the Bible, and they had the precepts of the Oxford Group (*DR. BOB and the Good Oldtimers* [New York: Alcoholics Anonymous World Services, 1980], p. 96).

> [Dr. Bob said:] We already had the basic ideas, though not in terse and tangible form. We got them . . . as a result of our study of the Good Book (*DR. BOB*, p. 97).

> Dr. Bob, noting that there were no Twelve Steps at the time . . . said they were convinced that the answer to their problems was in the Good Book. "To some of us older ones, the parts we found absolutely essential were the Sermon on the Mount [Matthew 5-7], the 13th chapter of First Corinthians, and the Book of James," he said (*DR. BOB,* p. 96).

> . . . the Book of James was a favorite with early A.A.'s [said Bill Wilson]–so much so that "The James Club" was favored by some as a name for the fellowship (*DR. BOB*, p. 71).

> [As to the Oxford Group influence:] Emphasis was placed on prayer and on seeking guidance from God in all matters. The movement also relied on study of the Scriptures and developed some of its own literature as well. At the core of the program were the "four absolutes": absolute honesty, absolute unselfishness, absolute purity, and absolute love (*DR. BOB*, p. 54).

> We had much prayer together in those days and began quietly to read Scripture and discuss a practical approach to its application in our lives (*DR. BOB*, p. 111).

> In November of 1937, Bill Wilson was in Akron. "Bill's writings record the day he sat in the living room with Doc, counting recoveries. 'A hard core of very grim, last-gasp cases had by then

been sober a couple of years,' he said. 'All told, we figured that upwards of 40 alcoholics were staying bone dry'" (*DR. BOB*, p. 123; see also *Lois Remembers*, pp. 107-08).

Meeting at T. Henry Williams's home in Akron, the alcoholics had a "long, hard-fought session. But together Bill and Bob persuaded a bare majority of 18 A.A.'s gathered at T. Henry's..." to accept Bill's package and allow Bill to write a book of experiences that would carry the message of recovery to other cities and other countries (*DR. BOB*, pp. 123-24).

Investigating the Akron "Program" in some depth, Frank Amos–later an A.A. trustee–reported to John D. Rockefeller, Jr., on the program's details (*DR. BOB*, p. 131-36).

With such a backdrop of recoveries and a developed "Program" that had worked for forty tough, "medically incurable" cases, Bill began writing his Big Book. He was fashioning a "how it worked" program from the Akron success with the Bible and the precepts of the Oxford Group. His suggested "path" certainly was not germinated by or supported by his own failures on the New York scene. (See Dick B., *Turning Point: A History of Early A.A.'s Roots and Successes*, pp. 109-16; *Lois Remembers*, pp. 95, 124.) There was not one warped or distorted word–in Wilson's earliest drafts–concerning Almighty God and a "higher power," a "power greater than ourselves," or "God as we understood Him." Not when Bill first started, that is. There was God! Creator. Maker. Spirit. Father. Yahweh–Who had been the subject of Bill's three months of Bible study with the Smiths at their home in Akron in the summer of 1935. Then things began to change–even as the drafts changed and were given new orientations by Bill. And Yahweh–Whose name was holy and not to be profaned–began to get new names and attributes affixed to Him by recovery theorists and revisionists.

Then Everybody Took a Crack at It. Now, over sixty-five years later, here is what others have said and fashioned about what

Bill meant to say about this program that worked and the Creator upon whom its adherents had placed their reliance.

- **Terence T. Gorski**

    [Step Two.] There is something more powerful than I that can help me to stop drinking. I can't, but **somebody else can** (Terrence T. Gorski, *Understanding The Twelve Steps: A Guide for Counselors, Therapists, and Recovering People* [Missouri: Herald House/Independence Press, 1989], p. 75; bold face added).

    In Step Two we develop a sense of faith that there is someone or something bigger and more powerful than we are. There is **someone or something out there** that knows more about addiction and about recovery than I do. There is someone out there that has the answer, someone who can tell me what to do to recover from my alcoholism. A "power greater" implies that **this "something" is greater than we are.** There are some people who claim that a **Higher Power can be anything, even a Coke bottle**. I personally have trouble with that (Gorski, *Understanding*, p. 95; bold face added).

- **Marianne W. Gilliam**

    A.A. correctly anticipated the problems they would encounter in placing reliance upon a Higher Power and so decreed that a **Higher Power could be anything we interpret it to be, even a tree**. However, the focus was still on something outside ourselves. But I was starting to discover that in order to find our own inner power we needed to find that personal aspect of God WITHIN us. . . . I believe we have God's energy manifesting in us every day of our lives (Marianne W. Gilliam, *How Alcoholics Anonymous Failed Me: My Personal Journey to Sobriety Through Self-Empowerment* [New York: William Morrow, 1998], p. 45; bold face added).

- **Saul Selby**

  AA'S STEP TWO: CHRISTIAN ADAPTATION: To experience Jesus as personal and available (Saul Selby, *Twelve Step Christianity: The Christian Roots and Application of the Twelve Steps* [MN: Hazelden Foundation, 2001], p. 25).

- **Morris E. Chafetz and Harold W. Demone, Jr.**

  If the alcoholic striving for sobriety can **turn his will over to AA** ("a new-found Providence"), he will begin moving in an appropriate direction. Although AA is mindful that dependence can be dangerous in therapeutic relations, it is their experience that dependence on an AA group or on a higher "Power" has not produced any disastrous results (Morris E. Chafetz and Harold W. Demone, Jr., *Alcoholism & Society* [NY: Oxford University Press, 1962], p. 150; bold face added).

- **Martin and Deidre Bobgan**

  The "Power greater than ourselves" can be **anybody or anything that seems greater** than the person who takes Step Two. It can be a familiar spirit., such as Carl Jung's Philemon. It could be any deity of Hindu-ism, Buddhism, Greek mythology, or New Age channeled entities. It could be one's own so-called higher self. It could even be the devil himself. The extreme naivete of Christians comes through when they confidently assert that their higher Power is Jesus Christ. Since when did Jesus align Himself with false gods? Since when has He been willing to join the Pantheon or the array of Hindu deities. Jesus is not an option of one among many. He is the Only Son, the Only Savior, and the Only Way (Martin and Deidre Bobgan, *12 Steps To Destruction: Codependency Recovery Heresies* [California: East Gate Publishers, 1991], p. 115; bold face added).

• **Philip Kavanaugh**

Spirituality in its simplest form is anything non-material. . . . To succeed in this healing journey, **we don't have to believe in God (meaning someone who pulls our strings)**. Recovery asks for a willingness to acknowledge that some power other than ourselves (the one who messed us up), whether that power is--Jesus Christ, Jehovah, **Buddha, Nature, Mighty Mouse**, or a nameless personal belief that there is a higher power that guides us (Philip Kavanaugh, M.D., *Magnificent Addiction* [Santa Rosa, CA: Aslan Publishing, 1992], p. 132; bold faced added).

Step Three. Finally we look beyond ourselves, to a power greater than ourselves, to whom we can surrender control. Someone who is totally trustworthy, totally dependable, totally loving, totally powerful, someone named with words such as "God," "Higher Power," "Allah," "Creative Life Source," or others. It does not matter whether we locate this power or presence in ourselves or in the heavens, whether we use the name of Nature, Jehovah, Christ, Mohammed, or Buddha, and whether we affiliate with a religious group or have only our own relationship with this Energy (Kavanaugh, *Magnificent Addiction*, p. 201).

• **Katherine Ketcham, et al.**

AA embodies a "spirituality of imperfection," which encourages alcoholics to look at themselves as they truly are and in that honest assessment discover not only humility but gratitude, tolerance, and forgiveness. Choose your own conception of God, and then let go of the demand for ultimate control: That philosophy forms the beating heart of A.A. . . . As long as you accept the fact that you are not God—then you are free to think of God in any way that you please (Ketcham, et al., *Beyond the Influence: Understanding and Defeating Alcoholism* [New York: Bantam Books, 2000], p. 204).

- **Ken Ragge**

  The reading of the sacred text [A.A.'s Big Book] is also a
  part of every meeting. The Oxford Group, being "more
  spiritual than religious," but still (in Christian countries)
  acknowledging its Christian roots, used the Bible for
  readings. Alcoholics Anonymous, being "spiritual, not
  religious," doesn't use the Bible at all; rather it uses another
  sacred text, the inspired Word of God as expressed through
  Bill Wilson, the Big Book. . . .Unlike the Oxford Group,
  which claimed salvation and redemption by Jesus through
  the Oxford Group, AA proclaims "recovery" by one's
  "Higher Power" through the Twelve Steps of Alcoholics
  Anonymous (Ken Ragge, *The Real AA: Behind the Myth of
  12-Step Recovery* [AZ: Sharp Press, 1998], pp. 82-83).

  Step Two, to the uninitiated, appears to be mostly about
  finding faith in God. While there may be some truth in this,
  working this Step is more a matter of **defining God in AA's
  image** (Ragge, *The Real AA*, p. 117; bold face added).

- **William L. Playfair, M.D.**

  They [the Twelve Steps] do not derive exclusively or even
  primarily from truths or concepts found in either the Old or
  New Testament. One cannot find anything even remotely
  similar to the Twelve Steps in the writings of ancient or
  modern Christian theologians. The secular nature of the
  Twelve Steps is, in fact, freely admitted by A.A. groups. Al-
  Anon, for instance, plainly asserts: The Twelve Steps . . .
  although spiritually oriented, are not based on a specific
  religious discipline. They embrace not only the philosophies
  of the Judeo-Christian faiths and the many religions of the
  East, but nonreligious, ethical and moral thought as well. .
  . As a matter of fact, AA's Twelve Steps are more akin to
  the Bahai faith than to Biblical Christianity (William L.
  Playfair, *The Useful Lie* [Illinois: Crossway Books, 1991],
  p. 87).

This *any* power of AA and the recovery industry is really just **that–any power, imagined or real**. Continuing its message to the clergy, AA concedes that: Some members of the clergy may be shocked to learn that an agnostic or an atheist may join the Fellowship, or to hear an AA [member] say: "I can't accept that 'God concept'; I put my faith in the AA group; that's my higher power, and it keeps me sober." The idea of the AA group as the Higher Power or god of an AA member should not be shrugged off as hypothetical or even all that exceptional. Recovery industry literature is replete with testimonials of this kind (Playfair, *The Useful Lie*, p. 91; bold face added).

- **Jan R. Wilson and Judith A. Wilson**

There are **many different ideas of a Higher Power**. The chapter on Step Two in Twelve Steps and Twelve Traditions describes several types of experiences with God before getting into a recovery program. Some are what one might call a traditional idea of God and some are very nontraditional. All that seems to be required is that the Higher **Power be someone or something that you can relate to that is more powerful than your addiction**. . . . Some people have such negative reactions to the traditional ideas that for a while they have to think of "GOD" as Good Orderly Direction, from wherever it comes. Some even say their Higher Power was just a **Group Of Drunks** (Jan R. Wilson and Judith A. Wilson, *Addictionary: A Primer of Recovery Terms and Concepts from Abstinence to Withdrawal* [New York: A Fireside/Parkside Recovery Book, 1992], pp. 181-82; bold face added).

- **Ernest Kurtz, Ph.D. and Katherine Ketcham**

The use of the phrase *Higher Power*–his, hers, yours, or mine–rather than the word *God*, reminds members of A.A.'s tolerance of individual differences in religious belief and spiritual inclination. The most basic understanding of the concept "Higher Power" within Alcoholics Anonymous is *that which keeps me sober*. In a sense, this is to out-James William James; it is the ultimate pragmatic concept of God. For alcoholics who have tried and failed time after time to stay sober by themselves, for alcoholics who have tried and failed after using any one of innumerable techniques, that which finally *does* keep one sober becomes "God" (Ernest Kurtz and Katherine Ketcham, *The Spirituality of Imperfection: Modern Wisdom from Classic Stories* [New York: Bantam Books, 1992], p. 208; bold face added).

- **Albert Ellis and Emmett Velten, Jr.**

Medicine and psychiatry in 1935 got nowhere with most problem drinkers. Clinical psychology, clinical social work, and counseling hardly existed. What could Bill Wilson and Dr. Bob Smith call upon for help but religion?. . . . **AA's answer for alcohol abusers was a simple form of spiritual healing through the Grace of God**, but without the trappings of formal religion and churches. Many twelve-step program followers (who abide by the twelve steps used in AA and other "Anonymous" groups) today make a distinction between spiritual and religious, as if religion were automatically a bad thing. However, **"the God part" is a big feature of AA and remains a major strength and attraction** (Albert Ellis and Emmett Velten, *When AA Doesn't Work for You: Rational Steps to Quitting Alcohol* [Fort Lee, NJ: Barricade Books, 1992], p. 79; bold face added).

But Where Did "It" Come From

Above, in the quotes, you have it all. From Yahweh to Something. From God to Group Of Drunks. From our Creator to Somebody Else. From Bible to Baloney. From Baptist to Bahai. From Bible-believing to power-greater-than-ourselves-ism!

I'll not spend much time on where "Power greater than ourselves" really came from. I just don't know. And, as usual, its author Bill Wilson didn't tell us. But it sure didn't come from God. And it sure didn't come from the Bible.

I feel quite free to assert that the ill-defined, mythical, distorted, utterly confusing "it" is the product of whole-cloth manufacture. A product fashioned by the combined forces of atheists, booksellers, salaried service writers, iconoclasts, uninformed clergy, misguided Christian writers, treatment programs, therapists, angry bleeding deacons, frustrated failures, and probably the just-plain-ignorant. But certainly not by Dr. Bob, nor Anne, nor Henrietta Seiberling, nor T. Henry or Clarace Williams! Not even by Bill Wilson in his wildest writing moments.

Yet I personally have heard *all* the weird names in the rooms of A.A. or read them in recovery literature; and–desperate for deliverance, recovery, and freedom–I picked up some of these bizarre appellations and really toyed with them for far too long. But no more! Today, I believe myself to be a certified, recovered, delivered, happy, joyous, free, Bible-studying, Christian, ex-real-alcoholic within the halls of Alcoholics Anonymous who believes in the one true living God and came to Him through His son Jesus Christ. Just think! Within the halls of A.A.! I don't have to worry about whether a radiator is a power or whether I even need to come to believe in or develop an understanding of radiators to get well.

When I finally plunged in to my Oxford Group research several years ago, I found the "Power greater" expression was in common usage in the Oxford Group, and probably was devised as a way of rejecting Biblical usage in favor of Buchman usage. (See the innumerable Oxford Group usages quoted in my title, *The Oxford Group and Alcoholics Anonymous*, pp. 341, 344, 346, 349, 362.) Something done in the Group without really intending to change the Bible itself. Something that would make Christianity "more appealing." That, of course, is something I don't think can or should be done. It gives rise to the same nonsense we have quoted above. But for your reading pleasure, here are some of the possible sources of the "power-greater-than-ourselves" language. Almost all, I believe, were written well before the Big Book was published in the Spring of 1939:

The Rev. Canon Samuel M. Shoemaker, Jr., D.D., S.T.D.–"Co-founder of A.A.":

A vast Power outside themselves (Shoemaker, *A Young Man's View of the* Ministry, p. 42).

A Force outside himself, greater than himself (Shoemaker, *If I Be Lifted Up*, p. 176).

Only God, therefore, can deal with sin. He must contrive to do for us what we have lost the power to do for ourselves (Shoemaker, *If I Be Lifted Up*, p. 133).

We talked of daily Quiet Time, of Bible study, prayer and listening, and of the power of God to lead and guide those who are obedient enough to be led (Shoemaker, *Children of the Second Birth*, pp. 148-49).

I have done wrong. I know I need to be changed, and I know some Power outside myself must do it (Shoemaker, *God and America*, p. 19).

Victor C. Kitchen–Oxford Group Writer, Colleague of Sam Shoemaker, Friend of Bill Wilson:

A power within yet coming from outside myself–a power far stronger than I was (Kitchen, *I Was a Pagan*, p. 63).

Higher Power (Kitchen, *I Was a Pagan*, p. 85).

It was this power of the Spirit flowing into me that . . . gave me not only the courage [but also] the strength . . . I needed (Kitchen, *I Was a Pagan*, p. 94).

It takes the power of God to remove these fears and mental conditions (Kitchen, *I Was a Pagan*, p. 143).

It takes the power of God to remove the desire for these indulgences (Kitchen, *I Was a Pagan,* p. 143).

Many did hesitate to call this force the "power of God" (Kitchen, *I Was a Pagan*, p. 16).

Stephen Foot, British Oxford Group Writer, Author of Best-selling "Life Began Yesterday":

New power and direction came to her when she started listening to God (Foot, *Life Began Yesterday*, p. 150).

This Power by which human nature can be changed . . . and through this Power problems are being solved (Foot, *Life Began Yesterday*, p. 22).

There is at work in the world today a Power that has for many generations been neglected by masses of mankind (Foot, *Life Began Yesterday*, p. 22).

I will ask God to show me His purpose for my life and claim from Him the power to carry that purpose out (Foot, *Life Began Yesterday*, p. 11).

Harold Begbie, Author of One of the Earliest, Popular Oxford Group Books:

The future of civilization, rising at this moment from the ruins of materialism, would seem to lie in an intelligent use by man of the ultimate source of spiritual Power (Begbie, *Life-Changers*, p. 22).

K. D. Belden–Longtime Oxford Group Leader and Writer:

Only the Power which raised Jesus Christ from the dead can, and
will, raise us from our old nature and begin to form in us the new
(Belden, *Reflections on Moral Re-Armament*, p. 28).

What a Ride!

I can and do speak for myself and perhaps for some other recovered
believers in A.A. who have been willing to apply reason to absurd
names for God. I've been taken on a royal ride. I came to A.A. sick,
sorry, bewildered, terrified, and guilty. I believed in God, and I still
do. I believed in what His Son Jesus Christ accomplished for me.
(See, for example: 1 Corinthians 1:30: "But of him are ye in Christ
Jesus, who of God is made unto us wisdom, and righteousness, and
sanctification, and redemption"; 1 Thessalonians 1:9-10: "For they
themselves shew of us what manner of entering in we had unto you,
and how ye turned to God from idols to serve the living and true God;
And to wait for his Son from heaven, whom he raised from the dead,
even Jesus, which delivered us from the wrath to come";1 Peter 2:24:
"Who his own self bare our sins in his own body on the tree, that we,
being dead to sins, should live unto righteousness: by whose stripes
ye were healed..")

And I still do believe in that deliverance, righteousness, and healing
that was accomplished for me. I believed that God's Word contained
the truth about these things, and I still do. But I have put out the
foregoing quotes by the theorists, just to show you how many
roadblocks appeared on my ride, confused me at the outset, resulted
in many an unfortunate diversion by A.A. friends, and caused me to
hold back in my work to help others. Now that I know just how much
nonsense has been poured into the "Power greater than ourselves"
mold, I'll never take, or invite anyone to take, that detour again. And,
to those, who offer a trip on the royal "something" or "any power" or
"group" train, I'll say *for* myself (and for those I try to help) *to* those
who are the engineers: "Jesus answered them and said unto them, Ye

do err, not knowing the scriptures, nor the power of God" (Matthew 22:29).

Bill and Bob were not selling snake oil. They were selling the good news in Scripture. And I bought that product–after an unneeded delay; and I was healed by the power of God *in* Alcoholics Anonymous, just like the forty pioneers were. You can also be healed. Your Heavenly Father will never let you down!

"God as we understood Him" An Alleged Compromise That Opened the Door

My Own Experience

At my first A.A. meeting, I was delighted. Friendliness, laughter, concern, suggestions. All came pouring toward me at the "Wednesday Night What It's Like Now" meeting-later to become my Home Group. At my second meeting, I made a speech about needing help with a pending court appearance. And a non-attorney offered to come with me; he said he had studied law in Brazil. By my third meeting, I was beginning to detox heavily. Yet I didn't know what detoxing was, what was happening, or that I was becoming really sick. They told me to use orange juice and honey. I searched high and low for honey, bought a bag of oranges, put them in the microwave, and never saw them again. But I made another speech.

This time, I stood at the door of the "Friday Nite Beginners' Meeting," announced that I had been very frightened, said I had seen "God as we understood Him" on the wall, had prayed to God as I did understand Him, and had really found peace, for that night at least. Unquestionably, however, I was a little crazy-as only A.A. newcomers can be. A few days later, I had three grand mal seizures at an A.A. meeting. I was trundled off in an ambulance to the Emergency Room and then Intensive Care. In a day or two, I checked in to a treatment center. But that's another story. The point here is that I stuck, and have stuck, with A.A. I believed I could and would receive help because A.A. had seemed to recommend entrusting my life to the care of God as I understood Him. I've since found out that thousands have done the same thing in the more than sixty-five years since A.A.'s founding. They, like myself, have received help. Some are simply "dry"-still suffering from "untreated alcoholism." Some say they are "in recovery." Some of us say we have "recovered," Some of us, just as Bill Wilson, Dr. Bob, and A.A. Number Three (Bill Dotson) said, say we have been "cured." Some of us, who are believers, are very clear that we have been delivered by our Heavenly Father from the power of darkness, translated into the kingdom of His dear Son, and made known to us the riches of the glory of the mystery–which is Christ in you, the hope of glory (Colossians 1:13, 27).

So, Was A.A. Really about God "as we understood Him"?

It didn't take very long for me to get an answer to that question. Of course it wasn't! And how did I find out. Well, I've already covered the myriad of "higher power" and "power greater than ourselves" phrases that were floating around the rooms and in recent Twelve Step literature. No rational person could say these have anything whatever to do with the Creator. These "powers" seemed to mean just about anything to the confused crowd with which I hung out. Whether my new-found A.A. friends had been lawyers like myself, painters like my first sponsor, warehousemen like his sponsor, teachers like my room mate, or "consultants" (a handy A.A. word for unemployed, devastated, newcomers), all had different ideas about this "power greater than themselves."

My first sponsor did occasionally talk about God. His sponsor talked about a "higher power." My roommate talked about witchcraft. Others talked about a "rock," a "Big Dipper," and a "Group of Drunks" as their higher powers. Some even offered to "loan" out their own "higher power" until the newer person could find his own-which, they said, could be anything greater than himself. One authoritative sounding fellow assured those present at almost any and every Friday Nite Beginners' Meeting, that his "higher power" was Ralph. Somehow, I was able to resist buying in to that one. However, his name for a god still rings loudly in my ear.

But, as my increasing period of sobriety droned forward, and my continued need for God's help multiplied by leaps and bounds, I determined that there was no "common solution" or agreement in the A.A. rooms where I was going daily. There clearly was no consensus as to "who" or "what" this so-called higher power was. There certainly was plenty of confusion and confused thinking. In fact, many an older member has simply said in my presence that he couldn't and didn't need to understand "it." Rather, that he just needed to keep his "program" very very simple. All you had to keep in mind, these members proclaimed, was: "Just don't drink. And go to meetings." I have had no trouble following that advice for years. But as one writer said, "Drinking's not the problem." And I realized that many of these keep-it-simple guys had rarely advanced to any understanding of God at all. Certainly not that they would admit to. Almost all had not read the Bible, gone to any church, or developed any interest whatever in "religion." They boasted about the abandonment of their old religion. They bragged about A.A.'s being "spiritual, but not religious" even though few had the slightest idea what any of that meant.

Where Did This Phrase Originate?

I won't quote or cite the circulating accounts about where this "as we understood Him" phrase came from. Many are wrong. Most are conflicting. In fact, until my research was under way, I had found no one that even mentioned the phrase in the same breath with A.A. The story tellers had simply ignored the very probable, real source-the Reverend Samuel Moor Shoemaker, Jr., Rector of Calvary Episcopal Church in New York.

Shoemaker had been a vibrant leader of the Oxford Group in America. He had long been a friend and supporter of Oxford Group Founder Frank Buchman. He even provided housing for the virtual American headquarters of the Oxford Group in Calvary House, next to his Calvary Church in New York. He allowed Dr. Buchman to live there when Buchman was in the New York area. And Shoemaker wrote dozens of Oxford Group books, pamphlets, and articles until he split in 1941 with Buchman, the Oxford Group's founder and leader.

Actually, you can find many words and phrases in Sam Shoemaker's books that seem to have been incorporated almost verbatim in Bill Wilson's Big Book, talks, and writings. Bill often sang the praises of Reverend Shoemaker, dubbed Sam a "Co-founder" of A.A., said Sam had been a well-spring of its ideas, exchanged lots of correspondence with Sam, and had him speak at two A.A. International Conventions. Sam was also invited to, and did, write several articles for A.A.'s "house organ," the *AA Grapevine*. Bill had many a talk with Sam Shoemaker before he (Bill) drafted A.A.'s basic text. Bill submitted a draft manuscript to Shoemaker for review prior to publication in 1939. And Bill had asked Sam Shoemaker to write the Twelve Steps. However, Shoemaker declined-saying the Steps should be written by an alcoholic, namely, Bill.

Shoemaker was the closest thing to a spiritual mentor that Bill Wilson had, prior to his completion and publication of A.A.'s Big Book in the Spring of 1939. Bill had never belonged to a church. He had (by his own acknowledgment) been a "conservative atheist." Bill has been reported, by his wife and by A.A.'s first archivist, to have read practically no religious literature. Bill himself said he knew nothing about the Bible until he moved in with Dr. Bob and Anne Smith in the summer of 1935-the period when A.A. was founded-and when Bill and Dr. Bob had conducted nightly discussions of the Bible and Oxford Group principles and practices.

The foregoing facts about Bill, A.A., and Sam Shoemaker can be found specifically documented in a number of writings. I have covered most all of them all in my title, *New Light on Alcoholism: God, Sam Shoemaker, and A.A.*, 2d ed. (http://www.dickb.com/newlight.shtml). I've also covered them in my titles about the Oxford Group and Shoemaker: *The Oxford Group and Alcoholics Anonymous: A Design for Living That Works* (http://www.dickb.com/Oxford.shtml) and *Good Morning!: Quiet Time, etc.* (http://www.dickb.com/goodmorn.shtml). I've discussed them as well in *Courage to Change* (a title I wrote with Bill Pittman) and in *The Akron Genesis of Alcoholics Anonymous*, 2d ed. (http://www.dickb.com/Akron.shtml). Wilson himself discussed most of these facts. They are recorded, here and there, in *Alcoholics Anonymous Comes of Age*, *The Language of the Heart*, *Pass It On*, and the *Best of the Grapevine* volumes (all being "Conference Approved"publications of Alcoholics Anonymous World Services).

Specific Examples in Shoemaker Writings of the "God as we understand Him" Idea

First, We Must Look at Surrender to God: Sam wrote much about the importance of surrender–surrender to God! Among his papers at the Episcopal Church Archives in Austin, Texas, I found the following:

> There was nothing actually new to be learned from the experience when related. "I just gave my life over to God" or "I surrender to Christ" (Dick B., *New Light on Alcoholism*, 2d ed., p. 92; [http://www.dickb.com/newlight.shtml]).

Other Examples of Sam's Surrender Language:

> Except a man be born again, he cannot see the kingdom of God. . . . A man is born again when the control of his life, its center and its direction pass from himself to God (Shoemaker, *National Awakening*, p. 57).

> One may say that the whole development of Christianity in inwardness has consisted in little more than the greater and

greater emphasis attached to this crisis of self-surrender (Shoemaker, *Realizing Religion*, p. 30).

Surrender is not conversion, we cannot convert ourselves; but it is the first step in the process (Shoemaker, *Confident Faith*, p. 41).

Sam on the Act of Surrender–a Decision:

Decision. . . . We must help people to make an act of self-surrender to Christ, which renounces all known sins, accepts Him as Saviour, and begins Christian life in earnest (Shoemaker, *The Church Alive*, p. 41).

He went into his room, knelt by his bed, and gave his life in surrender to God (Shoemaker, *Children of the Second Birth*, p. 175).

She surrendered to God her groundless fears, and with them turned over her life for His direction (Shoemaker, *Children of the Second Birth*, p. 82).

That night I decided to "launch out into the deep:" and with the decision to cast my will and my life on God, there came an indescribable sense of relief, of burdens dropping away (Shoemaker, *Twice-Born Ministers*, p. 134).

And Then, Said Sam, Surrender As Much of Yourself As You Can to As Much of God As You Understand:

So they prayed together, opening their minds to *as much of God as he understood.* . . . (Shoemaker, *Children of the Second Birth*, p. 47, italics added).

So he said that he would "surrender as much of himself as he could, to *as much of Christ as he understood*" (Shoemaker, *Children of the Second Birth*, p. 25; italics added. See also, and compare "In Memoriam" Princeton, *The Graduate Council*, June

10, 1956, pp. 2-3; and Shoemaker, *How to Become a Christian*, p. 72).

The finding of God, moreover, is a progressive discovery; and there is so much more for all of us to learn about him. (Shoemaker, *How to Find God*, p. 1).

Begin honestly where you are. Horace Bushnell once said, "Pray to the dim God, confessing the dimness for honesty's sake." I was with a man who prayed his first real prayer in these words: "O God, if there be a God, help me now because I need it." God sent him help. He found faith. He found God. . . God will come through to you and make Himself known (Shoemaker, *How to Find God*, p. 6. See and compare: *Alcoholics Anonymous*, 4th ed., p. 37: "But He has come to all who have honestly sought Him. When we drew near to Him. He disclosed Himself to us!" See also, in the Bible book so popular with the pioneers-James: "Draw nigh to God, and he will draw nigh to you," James 4:8).

[A]ny honest person can begin the spiritual experiment by surrendering "as much of himself as he can, to *as much of Christ as he understands*" (Shoemaker, *Extraordinary Living for Ordinary Men*, p. 76; italics added).

For a Christian, of course, the intellectual content concerns *Jesus Christ*. I believe we can start by *accepting as much of Him as we understand*, but I believe that continuous obedience toward Him and contact with Him will steadily convince us that shallow, humanistic interpretations of Him do not fit the facts. . . . I know many persons who have begun by surrendering as much of themselves as they can to *as much of Him as they understand* (Shoemaker, *The Experiment of Faith*, p. 26; italics added).

Shoemaker did not speak at all about surrendering to as much of Ralph or to as much of a lightbulb or to as much of a tree as you understand! A.A.'s Big Book implored: May you find God, Almighty God, our Creator–not just some A.A. group! A.A. Groups are found in meeting schedules, not in the Bible.

Said Sam in substance: You simply start where you are in your understanding. You surrender as much of yourself as you can. To as much of God as you understand. Then, added Sam, God will come through to you, make Himself known, and enable you to understand more. You will come to believe. You will find God, said Sam. God will make Himself known. God will not be making known a tree, a coke bottle, or a radiator. He will make known Himself and by name—God, the Creator, Yahweh!

Similar Ideas and Words in Other Oxford Group Writings

Stephen Foot was one of the most popular Oxford Group writers of the early 1930's. Foot used a slightly different form of expression. It presented the same idea of initial, limited understanding. It spoke not of *understanding*, but instead of initial, limited *knowledge* of God (surrendering all that you *know* of self to all that you *know of God*). Foot's language was also used by Dr. Bob's wife Anne Smith in her journal, and by long-time Oxford Group activist James D. Newton in his biographical *Uncommon Friends* title. These stalwart Oxford Group admirers were also readers of, and thoroughly acquainted with, the works of Rev. Sam Shoemaker. Respectively, they wrote:

> Life began for me with a surrender of all that I know of self to *all that I knew of God* (Foot, *Life Began Yesterday*, pp. 12-13; italics added. See also James D. Newton, *Uncommon Friends*, p. 154).

> Are you prepared to do his will, let the cost be what it may? That is surrender of all one knows of self to *all one knows of God* (Foot, *Life Began Yesterday*, p. 175; italics added).

> [In her journal, Dr. Bob's wife Anne Smith twice wrote the following idea:] Try to bring a person to a decision to "surrender as much of himself as he knows to *as much of God as he knows*." Stay with him until he makes a decision and says it aloud (Dick B., *Anne Smith's Journal*, 3rd ed, pp. 25, 97; italics added; [http://www.dickb.com/annesm.shtml]).

Look at What Bill Wilson Said before He Compromised with "Atheism":

Before he scratched out "God" in favor of his "as we understood Him" compromise language, Bill was telling the story far differently, far more accurately, and far more consistently in terms of what he had learned from his sponsor Ebby Thacher, from Dr. Bob, from Anne Smith and her journal, from Shoemaker, and from Oxford Group writings and talks. Bill wrote:

> This is what my friend [Ebby Thacher] suggested I do: Turn my face to God *as I understand Him* [italics added] and say to Him with earnestness-complete honesty and abandon-that I henceforth place my life at His disposal and Direction forever (*Bill Wilson's Original Story*, a thirty-four page document I found at Bill's home at Stepping Stones, p. 30, lines 989-992).

> [Ebby Thacher said to Bill:] *So, call on God as you understand God.* Try prayer (W.W., "The Fellowship of Alcoholics Anonymous," *Quarterly Journal of Studies on Alcohol* [Yale University, 1945], p. 463; italics added).

> [Reciting in A.A.'s own basic text, precisely how he had followed Ebby Thacher's instructions, Bill wrote:] There I humbly offered myself to *God, as I then understood Him*, to do with me as He would. I placed myself unreservedly under His care and direction (*Alcoholics Anonymous*, 4th ed., p. 13; italics added).

Bill did not turn his face to, or call on, or humbly offer himself to, a radiator, a tree, a lightbulb, a Group of Drunks, or any other blatantly idolatrous symbol. He turned to God as he (Bill Wilson) did then and there understand God. That is a piece of very easily understood, yet virtually ignored A.A. history that should be blazoned on the desk of everyone who tries to sell snake oil to an unwary A.A. newcomer.

Using language very similar to that used by Sam Shoemaker in his book *Confident Faith*, Bill wrote quite eloquently:

> When we became alcoholics crushed by a self-imposed crisis we could not postpone or evade, we had to fearlessly face the proposition that either God is everything or else He is nothing. God either is, or He isn't. What was our choice to be? (*Alcoholics Anonymous*, 4th ed., p. 53. See also Hebrews 11:6 ["... for he that cometh to God must believe that he is, and that he is a rewarder of them that diligently seek Him"]; and Shoemaker, *Confident Faith*, pp. 20-21 ["God is, or He isn't. You leap one way or the other"]).

Bill did not assert that a radiator either is or it isn't. He did not claim that a lightbulb either is or it isn't. He didn't declare that Santa Claus either is or he isn't. Consistent with the words of Hebrews 11:6 in the Bible, and the reasoning of his friend Sam Shoemaker, Bill Wilson made the very simple and rational statement that God either is, or He isn't. Then, following the instructions of the Oxford Group, Shoemaker, and his friend Ebby Thacher, Bill Wilson "surrendered as much of himself as he understood to as much of God as he (Bill) then understood."

You Start with Shoemaker, the Oxford Group, and Dr. Bob's Wife

That's it, folks. The story of how the "God as we understood Him" phrase came to be inserted in the Big Book and Twelve Steps; and the truth seems to have been much distorted by the claim of an A.A. old-timer Jim B. that he (Jim) was responsible for this phrase "as we understood Him." We thoroughly explored that claim, just as far as we were able; and we found that Bill Wilson had never acknowledged Jim's claim. As we researched Shoemaker's writings, Oxford Group books, the writings of Bill's secretary Ruth Hock, and Anne Smith's journal, we saw a far different history that suggested a far different origin of the phrase. For one thing, we saw that Jim B. had not been sober until long after Stephen Foot, Sam Shoemaker, Jim Newton, and Anne Smith had tendered the commonly used suggestion that you surrender to as much of God as you understand! Or know. (See Dick B., *Turning Point*, pp. 172-81 [http://www.dickb.com/Turning.shtml]; *Anne Smith's Journal*, 3rd ed., p.26, n.10 [http://www.dickb.com/annesm.shtml]).

You don't start with an avowed atheist (Jim B.) who apparently was neither sober nor present when the phrase "as we understood Him" was suggested and then substituted in Step Three and Step Eleven. You start with the Bible students (Sam Shoemaker and Anne Smith-Dr. Bob's wife) who were close to Bill Wilson in the pre-publication years and who had been expressing this idea five to ten years before A.A.'s Big Book was first published. These leaders did have an understanding of God. They felt others could gain an understanding and knowledge by starting with whatever understanding they had at the time of their "surrender" to God. Quite clearly, Bill and his friends were talking about God, the Creator, Yahweh!

From what I can observe, there appear to have been no "nonsense gods" (higher powers, powers greater than ourselves, or gods of one's own understanding) in Akron's spiritual recovery program as that program was observed, described, and reported by Rockefeller's investigator Frank Amos and by the Akron pioneers themselves.

5
The Opportunity

This very day, we, who are *in* A.A. and fully conversant with its roots and value, have an unusually important opportunity: (1) To offer others who are willing to trust Almighty God and clean house this dissertation on obtaining complete healing in the hands of God; (2) To amplify and restore to our hearts and minds a full knowledge of Pioneer A.A. and its real biblical tools for recovery; and (3) To give A.A. Credit for, and encourage the practice of what it did best in the early days–help people to find God, to change and correct their lives, and carry a message of deliverance to those still suffering. And there are some specific points to keep in mind as we tell the good news.

- *Remember the Principle of One Drunk Helping Another*

  Recognize the effectiveness of teaching about alcoholism and its solution by having drunks tell other drunks about their former problem, their victory, and the way out.

- *Rely upon God's Power, Not Merely Human Power*

  Re-introduce God Almighty to the recovery picture. To be ashamed of mentioning God, to ignore the Creator's power, to substitute false idols for the true and living Creator, to ridicule church affiliations and religious beliefs, is a mark of deterioration, not progress.

- *Recognize the Debilitating Effect of Money*

  Relieve society of the belief that money thrown into prohibition, pledges, therapy, penalization, incarceration, treatment programs, medical research, clergy conferences, alcoholism and addiction studies, new "self-help" groups, new church-centered catchall programs, and government intrusion can possibly replace the voluntary, determined, recovery efforts of hurting alcoholics and addicts themselves.

- *Applaud Science, Medicine, Research, and Religious Bodies Without Depending upon Them*

Confine burgeoning expenditures to real medical research, early hospitalization costs, and scientific studies; and reduce money's importance as a factor in prevention, treatment, recovery, and the sustenance of government, non-profit, business, and religious agencies.

- *Applaud the Necessity for, and Encourage, Religious Help–Not Ridicule It*

AAs didn't invent a religion or A.A.'s religious program. They borrowed it, with religious help, from the Bible, from religious literature, from churches, and from clergy. Reliance on God, Bible study, prayer, devotionals, Quiet Time, and reading were not A.A. products. They were *learned* necessities for those whose plight seemed hopeless.

- *Recognize the Value of Long-Term Rehabilitation through Whatever Aids Society Offers*

Religion, Church, Education, Medical Information, Physical restoration, Life-change, Vocational Rehabilitation, Job Acquisition Training, Exercise programs, Nutrition programs, Family counseling, Wholesome recreation programs–All have their place in rehabilitation of destroyed lives. The real alcoholic is usually deficient in almost all these features, and it takes the "tincture of time" to eliminate the deficits.

- *Spurn Monopolistic Attitudes and Litigation Ventures*

Applaud the entry and growth of alternative programs such as "secular" recovery, "Christ-centered recovery," and A.A. Bible Study groups as proof that A.A. has and wants no monopoly on God, no monopoly on recovery ideas, and no program that withdraws into a shell spawning, and inviting, its own rejection by science, medicine, or religion. End the present-day emphasis on copyright litigation, the banning of "forbidden" literature at meetings, and the promotion of atheistic, universal growth.

- *Spread the Word That Growth after Sobriety Means Return to "Normal," Godly Living*

Publicize the idea that "growth"–in recovery, in the spiritual life, and in individual lives–is not measured by how many meetings a member attends, how "single" in purpose a recovery group's mission is kept, or how long one has abstained from an addiction. It is measured by the quality of godly life a "recovered" and "delivered" person is actually enjoying in sobriety–individually, with his family, with his job, with his business, with his schools and churches, with his community, and in fellowship with his Creator.

- *Open the Doors to Religious, Moral, Social, and Other Values of the "Outside World"*

Open the structured doors of later A.A. sobriety, and encourage the flood of recovered and delivered people into new lives with religious groups, family groups, education groups, service groups, business groups, recreation groups, and community groups, to mention only a few. Life never began nor ended with A.A., but it can begin again through the auspices of A.A.

• *Return to the Concept That Family Counts*

The disintegration of family life, of marriage, and of family responsibility hasn't altered the value of those factors in a healthy life. The family emphasis existed in early A.A. in Akron and Cleveland. And it should exist in the recovery scene today. (See Dick B. *Hope: The Story of Geraldine D., Alina Lodge & Recovery.* [Kihei, HI: Tincture of Time Press, 1997].)

• *Eliminate the Impact of Forces That Are Opposing The Creator, Swallowing A.A., and Encouraging an Idolatrous Group Therapy Philosophy in Recovery Programs*

Avoid the two greatest destructive forces that can becloud the goodness of God and eliminate the effectiveness of A.A. in dealing with alcoholism:

First, that A.A. or any other "recovery" group should put on the blinders, reject religion and God, avoid dealing with other addictions, and eliminate outside help from clergy and medicine. A.A.'s "being friendly with our friends" is not enough. It wasn't in the 1930's, and it isn't now.

Second, that A.A. should delete, revise, "universalize," and encourage the cloning (into one fellowship) of a bunch of look-alike "neutral newcomers" who have actually entered a unique and recognizable religious society that gained widespread acclaim in the beginning for at least three major achievements.

–   Its astonishing successes through its special reliance on God Almighty.

- The lessons learned by alcoholics from their own failures and the unsuccessful efforts of other human beings and entities.

- The attraction such factors really offered to seemingly hopeless and helpless newcomers and their families.

People do not often reject medical help because of fear of being "doctor-bitten." Nor do they usually shelve their Bibles because of fear of being "clergy-bitten." Neither, I believe, will the helpless and hopeless alcoholic shun help from the Creator because of fear of being "God-bitten." At least, he won't leave A.A. because of a "God-bitten" fear if A.A. and society don't foster it. But it's begun to happen, and there's an opportunity to end it if we want to.

- A.A. can be an effective and representative part of the family of God in combating alcoholism if it retains the generous attitude it first manifested toward other "anonymous" groups, "self-help" groups, and "addiction" groups. People have often fled to these other groups as virtual black sheep because of ambiguity as to what A.A. was really offering and to whom. Either A.A. has something to offer in the "God" field, or it doesn't. If God heals alcoholism and AAs are clear in that belief, they can have an enormous impact on the attitudes of government, medicine, religion, and other agencies in determining just how much such entities will welcome the powerful "God-business" solution. That's a message AAs will be able to carry by reason of their own success stories, past, present, and future.

6
Why Bring up God–Again!

The Big Deal
God Loves, Delivers, Heals, Forgives, and Guides

There's no particular need to review Scripture again. But let's at least remember what the Bible says about what God is and can do. You can read it in your own Bible today, or you can take a look at the verses and the chapter headings in *The Runner's Bible*, which was so widely used in Pioneer A.A.

From the Good Book:

God is love (1 John 4:8). God loves (John 3:16). God delivers, heals, and forgives (Psalms 103). God guides (Isaiah 58:11). As Dr. Bob's wife noted in her journal–He wishes above all things that we prosper and be in health (3 John 2). And ". . . with God nothing shall be impossible" (Luke 1:37). Now that's quite an order–just made for the woes of an alcoholic. The Pioneers could and did read those things in their Good Books.

From Their Devotionals:

They could also see them affirmed, in somewhat brief form, in the chapters and verses in their *Runner's Bibles*: (Walk in Love; Rejoice Always; In everything give thanks; Fear not, only believe; Get wisdom, Get understanding; Ask and ye shall receive; He that is the greatest among you shall be your servant; Forgive and ye shall be forgiven; Be of good cheer, thy sins be forgiven thee; I will help thee; Behold, I will heal thee; For thine is the power; The Lord shall guide thee continually; Thou shalt walk in thy way safely; All things are yours; Peace be unto you; Happy shalt thou be; and The Lord will lighten my darkness).

The pertinent verses and the chapters are all there too. They're still there. They covered the waterfront. AAs studied them, believed them, and apparently experienced their truth. Otherwise, why would they place such stock in the Good Book! Just read the stories in the Big Book's First Edition of 1939.

Let me tell you about my doctors here in Hawaii. When I seemed to be coming close to death in heart surgery last year in Honolulu, I told my surgeon that my family and I would be reading the Bible and praying a great deal. I asked him if that would be OK. He said, "We'll take all the help we can get." When I first met my cardiologist on Maui and mentioned my A.A. involvement, he said, "It's the only thing that works." When I first met my dermatologist in Maui, I learned of his Christian beliefs and interest in my A.A. work. And then there was the approving smile from my general practitioner in California who said of A.A.: "Oh yes, they emphasize the religious, don't they? I wish the man in my outer office would go to them for his drinking problem as you have." My anesthesiologist in California was not only *in A.A.*, but he had recovered and returned to his Roman Catholic church. He was the A.A. sponsor of my opthamologist, who had not only recovered in A.A. but graciously contributed support to the publication of one of my titles. Now, I don't claim the entire medical profession is jumping up and down with excitement over A.A. But I can tell you I haven't run into any one of them myself who has told me to put down my Bible, forget Jesus Christ, and let go to something or somebody other than God.

These physicians, like many clergymen, may have their questions about A.A. repeaters and relapsers, but they're not running around proposing higher powers that are radiators, flower pots, or rainbows. They are not suggesting that alcoholics turn their lives over to the care of these inanimate objects.

The "Higher Power" Theology
Just Hasn't Been That Good!

There are plenty in recovery groups today that get rabid when there's talk of God, the Bible, or Christianity. But their substitute nonsense is shabby and unconvincing. There is no need here to cover all the researchers, scholars, writers, and critics who have commented on today's dismal success rates and repeated relapses. You can find the remarks of many in Appendix Three of my latest title *Why Early A.A. Succeeded: The Good Book in Alcoholics Anonymous Yesterday and Today* (Kihei, HI: Paradise Research Publications, 2001), pp. 267-93. You can find some earlier documented remarks in Appendix Twelve of the second edition of my Shoemaker title, *New Light on Alcoholism*, pp. 569-74. The commentators include government leaders, scientists, physicians, psychologists, clergymen, atheists, and secular recovery advocates, among others.

The following woman critic is just one of the many mentioned above:

> I did a bit of research into A.A. and other twelve-step groups and was startled by what I discovered. Although A.A. is the most successful program for achieving sobriety, its relapse rate shocked me. Let me give you some overall all statistics about alcoholism. Of the estimated 14 million adult Americans who are deemed alcoholic, less than 10 percent of them will be seeking help at any given time. Of those 10 percent, 70 percent won't achieve lasting sobriety. Seventy percent of those who achieve sobriety in A.A. will relapse within five years. The relapse rates for one year are even higher. So for long-term sobriety, only 3 percent of all adult alcoholics will successfully quit drinking by using A.A. Three percent! (Calculated as 30 percent of the 10 percent of the entire drinking population who are seeking help). (Marianne G. Gilliam, *How Alcoholics Anonymous Failed Me: My Personal Journey to Sobriety through Self-Empowerment* [New York: Eagle Brook, 1998], p. xviii.)

Analysts of "Divine Help"
Are Neither Numerous, United, Nor Persuasive

Those who have a problem with God in the recovery picture are often atheists. Charles Bufe–whose *Alcoholics Anonymous: Cult or Cure?* (San Francisco: Sharp Press, 1991) has attracted much attention and been revised and reprinted–stated to me he was an atheist. Some commentators just describe themselves as "not religious;" and Dr. Stanton Peele, author of the much-quoted *Diseasing of America*, told me he was one of these. Others have simply left behind their religious ties as ministers or priests; and Dr. Ernest Kurtz, author of *Not-God*, is one of these. Still others are desirous of escaping the rigors of Christianity and removing themselves from any A.A. scene that seems to demand it. Marianne G. Gilliam (quoted above) could probably be counted among these–expressing enthusiasm over New Age. (See particularly, *How Alcoholics Anonymous Failed Me*, p. 222.) Some have simply observed that what they call "spirituality," and what I call the power of God, in the alcoholism arena has not been adequately addressed, researched, or measured.

Richard L. Gorsuch might be identified as one of these. He wrote Chapter 17 of *Research on Alcoholics Anonymous*, pp. 301-18. He titled his work "Assessing Spiritual Variables in Alcoholics Anonymous Research." Among the points he made are these:

> Despite the importance of spirituality in Alcoholics Anonymous' (AA) 12 steps, addiction research has seldom measured spirituality (p. 301).

> Spirituality. . . appears to be referring to people who are concerned with metaphysical issues as well as their day-to-day lives. It need have no belief in God. Little research has been done with this construct and so there is no real tradition of measurement with it. . . . But what is spirituality if it is entirely outside of a traditional religious focus, and does this spirituality relate to the Alcoholics Anonymous "Higher Power"? (p. 304).

In terms of psychological research, God concept studies show traditional Christians see God as kind, loving, and benevolent–but the alcoholics completely miss this. They would score high on another God concept factor: wrathfulness, *which is unrelated to the classical concept of the Christian God* (Spilka et al., 1985). Hence psychologically as well as theologically the "Christianity" of alcoholics is not the Christianity of most other American Christians. Alcoholics have a non-Christian view of God. How could this have come to be? . . . In my perspective there is a difference between "lip service" spirituality and involving spiritual resources in a program. . . . Lai (1982) interviewed 13 facilities in the Los Angeles area regarding both "lip service" to and the use of spirituality in their treatment programs. . . . Lai's programs showed the same sense of ambiguity regarding spiritual institutions that are found in A.A. and its programs: a rejection of institutional religion and acceptance of spirituality. . . . making such a strong split between classical religious institutions and spirituality encourages people to ignore the ready resources of their own traditions that could truly help in their spiritual development (pp. 310-13).

At about the foregoing point in Gorusch's comments, I was ready to climb off the Gorsuch train and invite others to do likewise. Gorsuch appears too mixed up with diverse ideas of religion, spirituality, higher power, steps, religious institutions, Christianity, and the "Christian God." He is just plain arrogant in his assertion that "alcoholics have a non-Christian view of God." But he makes the point in his conclusion that "there are many ways that spirituality could become truly manifest within AA programs and therefore could test whether the spirituality in the steps are helpful" (p. 314). Writing as though AAs are voluntary "specimens" for research, he mentions providing for each AA participant to be also a participant in a spiritually oriented organization of their choice simultaneously with involvement in A.A. The participant would be urged to attend worship services, participate in Bible studies, meet with a mentor for spiritual guidance, go to prayer meetings, participate in meditation, and go to special retreats, with spirituality as the prime goal of the meetings (pp. 314-15).

If the A.A. specimens were *also* provided with early A.A. history (which they are not), I'd find such suggestions somewhat palatable, somewhat in progress right now, and somewhat promising. Though quite impossible. But who would eliminate the hate remarks that presently accompany some of these efforts?

It seems fair to say that a real examination of the effectiveness of Divine Help, which was so loudly proclaimed in connection with early A.A., has not been the focus of significant measurement or evaluation in the recovery writings. And perhaps it cannot or should not be. The reason is that without a belief in Yahweh, acceptance that Jesus Christ is the only "way" to a relationship with the Creator, and measuring results in terms of Biblical truths, there would be little universal help to Christians, Jews, Moslems, atheists, and others at all. You'd spend all your time defining "spirituality" in terms of various beliefs and unbeliefs instead of relying on the miraculous work of the Creator. And you'd certainly be ignoring the Bible's warning about "natural man" reasoning. (See 1 Cor. 2:14.)

There is Healing in That "Old Time Religion"

Who's afraid of God? Treatment centers? Therapists? Physicians? Uncle Sam? Insurance Companies? Statisticians? Constitutional lawyers? I'd like to think it's only when they don't give Him their trust. "Fear not, only believe" was a common expression in early A.A. The Pioneers talked of "Divine Aid." They talked of the Bible. They talked of Jesus Christ. They talked of the Sermon on the Mount. They talked of the Book of James. They talked of 1 Corinthians 13. They talked of the Ten Commandments and the two "Great commandments" to love God and love your neighbor. They talked of Psalms, Proverbs, the Gospels, Acts, and love. And they got well and stayed well–for years, and years! Large percentages of them too.

The thesis here is that expressions like" "Let go and let God," "But for the grace of God." "There is One who has all power. That One is God," "God could and would if He were sought," " we are going to talk about God," "Creator," "Maker," "Almighty God," "Good Book," "God is love," "Thy will be done" and "cure" need to be headliners again in recovery discussions–even when the M.D.'s, D.D.'s, D.Min.'s, Ph.D.'s, M.A.'s, M.S.W.'s, and other "degreed" observers may not fully understand the words or expressions. The "natural man" may never understand them!

In almost all the foregoing writings I have discussed, you cannot find one single *adequate* explanation of either alcoholism or sin or disease or how God can help the alcoholic. And you don't need to.

God performs signs, wonders, and miracles. These works of God are "wonders." These are "miracles." The Bible didn't explain the "how" of it. But it did explain the "Who" of it. ". . . With men this is impossible; but with God all things are possible" (Matthew 19:26). "For with God nothing shall be impossible" (Luke 1:37). "Therefore I say unto you, What things soever ye desire, when ye pray, believe that ye receive them, and ye shall have them" (Mark 11:24). "For I am the Lord that healeth thee" (Exodus 15:26). ". . . Who healeth all thy diseases" (Psalm 103:3). You can find these and many other important verses quoted in *The Runner's Bible* and in *New Light on Alcoholism*, 2d ed., p. 23).

Rev. Sam Shoemaker, whom Bill called a "co-founder" of A.A., had it just right in the following statements (*By the Power of God* [New York: Harper & Brothers, 1954]):

> We can all have a share in letting such miracles [as the healing of the little boy] happen, if we link ourselves to the living power of God (p. 18).

The Source of spiritual power is God. . . . [I]t is His power, not ours, that does the wonderful things that spiritual power accomplishes for this world (pp. 30-31).

Faith . . . always thinks and feels positively, not negatively. It trusts God completely to be able to bring about His will (p. 134).

There may be much misgiving and great spiritual struggle somewhere: there must always be a great "giving in" that abandons self-generated power for God's power (p. 134).

In his 1863 Proclamation, President Abraham Lincoln said:

We have grown in numbers, wealth, and power as no other nation has ever grown. But we have forgotten God. . . . Intoxicated with unbroken success, we have become too self-sufficient to feel the necessity of redeeming and preserving grace, too proud to pray to the God that made us!

Is that what has happened to the Creator's power in the alcoholism battle? That's for each of us to decide, but I believe its simply too costly to pursue any path but the path to a relationship with the Creator. We who have paid our dues in self destruction, and who have had others watching helplessly by, simply have to have that kind and degree of power. We simply can't afford to forget God. Perhaps that's why our new President, George W. Bush, ends virtually every address today with "God Bless America." He means it, and that's just the kind of blessing we need to hear and have. God bless the alcoholic. God bless the addict. God has blessed millions of His kids, thousands of AAs, and yours truly. He can and will bless you if you seek Him.

I thank God that I sought His love, healing, deliverance, and forgiveness many years ago. Bill Wilson, in some of his better writing days, said: "God either is, or He isn't." Show me how I would have wound up if I had believed He *isn't*. One of my sponsees attended an A.A. conference with me in Sacramento, California, and stayed up most of the night in order to attend a certain marathon meeting. The meeting was titled, "God either is, or He isn't." I asked the sponsee what inspirational message he had received from the meeting. He replied, "Nothing." The problem, he said, was, "He *wasn't*." To allay his dismay, I left him, and I leave you, with this verse:

The fool hath said in his heart, there *is* no God. (Ps. 14:1)

End

Bibliography

Alcoholics Anonymous

Publications About

Alcoholics Anonymous. (multilith volume). New Jersey: Works Publishing Co., 1939.

Alcoholics Anonymous: The Story of How More Than 100 Men Have Recovered from Alcoholism. New York City: Works Publishing Company, 1939.

B., Dick. *Anne Smith's Journal, 1933-1939: A.A.'s Principles of Success.* 3rd ed. Kihei, HI: Paradise Research Publications, 1998.

———. *The Oxford Group & Alcoholics Anonymous: A Design for Living That Works.* 3d ed. Kihei, HI: Paradise Research Publications, 1998.

———. *Dr. Bob and His Library: A Major A.A. Spiritual Source.* 3rd ed. Kihei, HI: Paradise Research Publications, 1998.

———. *New Light on Alcoholism: God, Sam Shoemaker, and A.A., 2d ed..* Kihei, HI: Paradise Research Publications, 1999.

———. *That Amazing Grace: The Role of Clarence and Grace S. in Alcoholics Anonymous.* San Rafael, CA: Paradise Research Publications, 1996.

———. *The Akron Genesis of Alcoholics Anonymous.* 3rd ed. Kihei, HI: Paradise Research Publications, 1998.

———. *The Books Early AAs Read for Spiritual Growth.* 7th ed., Kihei, HI, CA: Paradise Research Publications, 1998.

———. *The Good Book and The Big Book: A.A.'s Roots in the Bible.* 2d ed., Kihei, HI: Paradise Research Publications, 1997.

———, and Bill Pittman. *Courage to Change: The Christian Roots of the 12-Step Movement.* Grand Rapids, MI: Fleming H. Revell, 1994.

———. *Turning Point: A History of Early A.A.'s Spiritual Roots and Successes.* Kihei, HI: Paradise Research Publications, 1997.

———. *Good Morning! Quiet Time, Morning Watch, Meditation, and Early A.A..* 2d ed. Kihei, HI: Paradise Research Publications, 1998.

———. *Utilizing Early A.A.'s Spiritual Roots for Recovery Today.* Kihei, HI: Paradise Research Publications, 1998.

———. *The Golden Text of A.A.: Early A.A., God, and Real Spirituality.* Kihei, HI: Paradise Research Publications, 1999.

———. *By the Power of God: A Guide to Early A.A. Groups & Forming Similar Groups Today.* Kihei, HI: Paradise Research Publications, 2000.

———. *Making Known the Biblical History and Roots of Alcoholics Anonymous.* Kihei, HI: Paradise Research Publications, 2001.

———. *Why Early A.A. Succeeded: The Good Book in A.A. Yesterday and Today.* Kihei, HI: Paradise Research Publications, 2001.

———. *Hope! The Story of Geraldine D., Alina Lodge, & Recovery.* Kihei, HI: Tincture of Time Press, 1997.

B., Jim. *Evolution of Alcoholics Anonymous*. New York: A.A. Archives.

Bishop, Charles, Jr. *The Washingtonians & Alcoholics Anonymous*. WV: The Bishop of Books, 1992.

C., Stewart. *A Reference Guide to the Big Book of Alcoholics Anonymous*. Seattle: Recovery Press, 1986.

Clapp, Charles, Jr. *Drinking's Not the Problem*. New York: Thomas Y. Crowell, 1949.

Conrad, Barnaby. *Time Is All We Have*. New York: Dell Publishing, 1986.

Darrah, Mary C. *Sister Ignatia: Angel of Alcoholics Anonymous*. Chicago: Loyola University Press, 1992.

E., Bob. *Handwritten note to Lois Wilson on pamphlet entitled "Four Absolutes."* (copy made available to the author at Founders Day Archives Room in Akron, Ohio, in June, 1991).

———. Letter from Bob E. to Nell Wing. Stepping Stones Archives.

First Steps: Al-Anon . . . 35 Years of Beginnings. New York: Al-Anon Family Group Headquarters, 1986.

Fitzgerald, Robert. *The Soul of Sponsorship: The Friendship of Father Ed Dowling, S.J., and Bill Wilson in Letters*. Center City, Minn.: Hazelden, 1995.

Ford, Betty, with Chris Chase. *The Times of My Life*. New York: Harper and Row, 1978.

Ford, John C. *Depth Psychology, Morality and Alcoholism*. Massachusetts: Weston College, 1951.

Gray, Jerry. *The Third Strike*. Minnesota: Hazelden, 1949.

Hunter, Willard, with assistance from M. D. B. *A.A.'s Roots in the Oxford Group*. New York: A.A. Archives, 1988.

Knippel, Charles T. *Samuel M. Shoemaker's Theological Influence on William G. Wilson's Twelve Step Spiritual Program of Recovery*. Ph. D. dissertation. St. Louis University, 1987.

Kurtz, Ernest. *Not-God: A History of Alcoholics Anonymous*. Exp. ed. Minnesota: Hazelden, 1991.

———. *Shame and Guilt: Characteristics of the Dependency Cycle*. Minnesota: Hazelden, 1981.

Morreim, Dennis C. *Changed Lives: The Story of Alcoholics Anonymous*. Minneapolis: Augsburg Fortress, 1991.

Morse, Robert M, M.D., and Daniel K. Flavin, M.D. "The Definition of Alcoholism." *The Journal of the American Medical Association*. August 26, 1992, pp. 1012-14.

P., Wally. *But, for the Grace of God . . .: How Intergroups & Central Offices Carried the Message of Alcoholics Anonymous in the 1940s*. West Virginia: The Bishop of Books, 1995.

Pittman, Bill. *AA The Way It Began*. Seattle: Glen Abbey Books, 1988.

Poe, Stephen E. and Frances E. *A Concordance to Alcoholics Anonymous*. Nevada: Purple Salamander Press, 1990.

Robertson, Nan. *Getting Better Inside Alcoholics Anonymous*. New York: William Morrow & Co., 1988.

S., Clarence. *Going through the Steps*. 2d ed. Altamonte Springs, FL: Stephen Foreman, 1985.

———. *My Higher Power—The Lightbulb*. 2d ed. Altamonte Springs, FL: Stephen Foreman, 1985.

Seiberling, John F. *Origins of Alcoholics Anonymous*. (A transcript of remarks by Henrietta B. Seiberling: transcript prepared by Congressman John F. Seiberling of a telephone conversation with his mother, Henrietta in the spring of 1971): Employee Assistance Quarterly. 1985; (1); pp. 8-12.

Sikorsky, Igor I., Jr. *AA's Godparents*. Minnesota: CompCare Publishers, 1990.

Smith, Bob and Sue Smith Windows. *Children of the Healer*. Illinois: Parkside Publishing Corporation, 1992.

Thomsen, Robert. *Bill W*. New York: Harper & Row, 1975.

Walker, Richmond. *For Drunks Only*. Minnesota: Hazelden, n.d.

———. *The 7 Points of Alcoholics Anonymous*. Seattle: Glen Abbey Books, 1989.

Webb, Terry. *Tree of Renewed Life: Spiritual Renewal of the Church through the Twelve-Step Program*. New York: Crossroad, 1992.

Wilson, Bill. *How The Big Book Was Put Together*. New York: A.A. General Services Archives, Transcript of Bill Wilson Speech delivered in Fort Worth, Texas, 1954.

———. *Bill Wilson's Original Story*. Bedford Hills, New York: Stepping Stones Archives, n.d., a manuscript whose individual lines are numbered 1 to 1180.

———. "Main Events: Alcoholics Anonymous Fact Sheet by Bill." November 1, 1954. Stepping Stones Archives. Bedford Hills, New York.

———. "The Fellowship of Alcoholics Anonymous." *Quarterly Journal of Studies on Alcohol*. Yale University, 1945, pp. 461-73.

———. *W. G. Wilson Recollections*. Bedford Hills, New York: Stepping Stones Archives, September 1, 1954 transcript of Bill's dictations to Ed B.

Wilson, Jan R., and Judith A. Wilson. *Addictionary: A Primer of Recovery Terms and Concepts from Abstinence to Withdrawal*. New York: Simon and Schuster, 1992.

Wilson, Lois. *Lois Remembers*. New York: Al-Anon Family Group Headquarters, 1987.

Windows, Sue Smith. (daughter of A.A.'s Co-Founder, Dr. Bob). Typewritten Memorandum entitled, *Henrietta and early Oxford Group Friends, by Sue Smith Windows*. Delivered to the author of this book by Sue Smith Windows at Akron, June, 1991.

Wing, Nell. *Grateful to Have Been There: My 42 Years with Bill and Lois, and the Evolution of Alcoholics Anonymous*. Illinois: Parkside Publishing Corporation, 1992.

Publications Approved by Alcoholics Anonymous

Alcoholics Anonymous. 4th ed. New York: Alcoholics Anonymous World Services, 2001

Alcoholics Anonymous. 3rd ed. New York: Alcoholics Anonymous World Services, 1976.

Alcoholics Anonymous. 1st ed. New Jersey: Works Publishing, 1939.

Alcoholics Anonymous Comes of Age. New York: Alcoholics Anonymous World Services, 1957.

A Newcomer Asks . . . York, England: A.A. Sterling Area Services, n.d.

As Bill Sees It: The A.A. Way of Life . . . *selected writings of A.A.'s Co-Founder*. New York: Alcoholics Anonymous World Services, 1967.

Best of the Grapevine. New York: The A.A. Grapevine, Inc., 1985.

Best of the Grapevine, Volume II. New York: The A.A. Grapevine, Inc., 1986.

Came to Believe. New York: Alcoholics Anonymous World Services, 1973.

Daily Reflections. New York: Alcoholics Anonymous World Services, 1991.

DR. BOB and the Good Oldtimers. New York: Alcoholics Anonymous World Services, 1980.

44 Questions. New York: Works Publishing, Inc., 1952.

Members of the Clergy Ask about Alcoholics Anonymous. New York: Alcoholics Anonymous World Services, 1961, 1979-revised 1992, according to 1989 Conference Advisory Action.

Pass It On. New York: Alcoholics Anonymous World Services, 1984.

Questions & Answers on Sponsorship. New York: Alcoholics Anonymous World Services, 1976.

The A.A. Grapevine: "RHS"—issue dedicated to the memory of the Co-Founder of Alcoholics Anonymous, DR. BOB. New York: A.A. Grapevine, Inc., 1951.

The A.A. Service Manual. New York: Alcoholics Anonymous World Services, 1990-1991.

The Co-Founders of Alcoholics Anonymous. New York: Alcoholics Anonymous World Services, 1972.

The Language of the Heart. Bill W.'s Grapevine Writings. New York: The A.A. Grapevine, Inc., 1988.

This is A.A. . . . An Introduction to the A.A. Recovery Program. New York: Alcoholics Anonymous World Services, 1984.

Twelve Steps and Twelve Traditions. New York: Alcoholics Anonymous World Services, 1953.

Pamphlets Circulated in Early A.A.

A.A. God's Instrument. Chicago: Chicago Area Alcoholics Anonymous Service Office, 1954.

A. A. Sponsorship: Its Opportunities and Its Responsibilities. Cleveland: Cleveland Ohio District Office, 1944.

A Guide to the Twelve Steps of Alcoholics Anonymous. Akron: AA of Akron, n.d.

A Guide to Serenity. Cleveland: The Cleveland District Office of Alcoholics Anonymous, n.d.

Alcoholics Anonymous: An Interpretation of our Twelve Steps. Washington, D.C.: Paragon Creative Printers, 1944.

A Manual for Alcoholics Anonymous. Akron: AA of Akron, n.d.

Central Bulletin, Volumes I - III. Cleveland Central Committee, October, 1942 - December, 1945.

Delahanty, Edward J., M.D. *The Therapeutic Value of the Twelve Steps of A.A.* Salt Lake City, UT: Alcoholism Foundations, n.d.

G., Clyde. *My Quiet Time.* Cleveland: Alcoholics Anonymous, n.d.

Handles and Hodge Podge, comp. a member of Alcoholics Anonymous. Cleveland: The Cleveland District Office of Alcoholics Anonymous, n.d.

Handles for Sobriety, comp. A Member of Alcoholics Anonymous. Cleveland: The Cleveland District Office of Alcoholics Anonymous, n.d.

"It's All in the Mind" Chicago: Chicago Area Alcoholics Anonymous Service Office, n.d.

Second Reader for Alcoholics Anonymous. Akron: AA of Akron, n.d.

Smith, Roy. *Emergency Rations.* Cleveland: The Cleveland District Office of Alcoholics Anonymous, n.d.

Spiritual Milestones in Alcoholics Anonymous. Akron: A.A. of Akron, n.d.

The New Way of Life: A.A. Cleveland: The Cleveland District Office of Alcoholics Anonymous, n.d.

T., John. *A.A.: God's Instrument.* Chicago: Chicago Area Alcoholics Anonymous Service Office, n.d.

The Devil and A.A. Chicago: Chicago Area Alcoholics Anonymous Service Office, 1948.

The Four Absolutes. Cleveland: Cleveland Central Committee of A.A., n.d.

The New Way of Life: A.A. Cleveland: The Cleveland District Office of Alcoholics Anonymous, n.d.

Twelve Steps of AA and The Bible. From the collection of Clancy U., n.d.

What Others Think of A.A. Akron: Friday Forum Luncheon Club, circa 1941.

Wood, Charles L. *Prayers for Alcoholics.* Cincinnati: Foreword Movement Publications, n.d. From a Midwest Intergroup Office.

Alcoholics Anonymous: Pro, Con, and Evaluated

A Program for You: A Guide to the Big Book's Design for Living. Hazelden Foundation, 1991.

B., Mel. *New Wine: The Spiritual Roots of the Twelve Step Miracle.* Hazelden Foundation, 1991.

Baker, John. *Celebrate Recovery.* Lake Forest, CA: Celebrate Recovery Books, 1994.

Bartosch, Bob and Pauline. *A Bridge to Recovery.* La Habra, CA: Overcomers Outreach, Inc., 1994.

Bishop, Charlie, Jr. and Pittman, Bill. *To Be Continued...The Alcoholics Anonymous World Biography 1935-1994.* Wheeling, WV: The Bishop of Books, 1994.

Bobgan, Martin and Deidre. *12 Steps to Destruction: Codependency Recovery Heresies.* Santa Barbara, CA: EastGate Publishers, 1991.

Bufe, Charles. *Alcoholics Anonymous: Cult or Cure?* 2d ed. AZ: Sharp Press, 1998.

Burns, Dr. Cathy. *Alcoholics Anonymous Unmasked: Deception and Deliverance.* Mt. Carmel, PA: Sharing, 1991.

Burns, Robert E., C.S.P. *The Catholic Church and Alcoholics Anonymous.* Columbia, 31: 15-16, May, 1952.

C., Chuck. *A New Pair of Glasses.* Irvine, CA: New-Look Publishing Company, 1984.

Catanzaro, Ronald J. *Alcoholism: The Total Treatment Approach.* IL: Charles C. Thomas Publisher, 1968.

Chafetz, Morris E., and Harold W. Demone, Jr. Alcoholism and Society. New York: Oxford University Press, 1962.

Chambers, Cal. *Two Tracks-One Goal: How Alcoholics Anonymous Relates to Christianity.* Langley, B.C., Canada: Credo Publishing Corporation, 1992.

Clinebell, Howard. *Understanding and Counseling Persons with Alcohol, Drug, and Behavioral Addictions.* Rev. and enl. ed. Nashville: Abingdon Press, 1998.

_____. *Well Being: A Personal Plan for Exploring and Enriching the Seven Dimensions of Life.* NY: HarperSan Francisco, 1992.

Costantino, Frank. *Holes in Time: The Autobiography of a Gangster.* 2d ed. Dallas, TX: Acclaimed Books, 1986.

Cunningham, Loren. *Is That Really You, God?: Hearing the Voice of God.* Seattle, WA: YWAM Publishing, 1984.

Davis, Martin M. *The Gospel and the Twelve Steps: Developing a Closer Relationship with Jesus*. San Diego, CA: Recovery Publications, 1993.

Dowling, The Reverend Edward, S.J. *Catholic Asceticism and the Twelve Steps*. St. Louis, MO, The Queen's Work, Brooklyn, 1953.

Doyle, Paul Barton. *In Step with God: A Scriptural Guide for Practicing 12 Step Programs*. Brentwood, TN: New Directions, 1989.

Dunn, Jerry G. *God is for the Alcoholic*. Chicago: Moody Press, 1965.

Ellis, Albert, and Emmett Belten. *When A.A. Doesn't Word for You: Rational Steps to Quitting Alcohol*. Fort Lee, NJ: Barricade Books, 1992.

Fingarette, Herbert. *Heavy Drinking: The Myth of Alcoholism as a Disease*. Berkeley, CA: University of California Press, 1988.

Fitzgerald, Robert. *The Soul of Sponsorship: The Friendship of Fr. Ed Dowling, S.J. and Bill Wilson in Letters*. Hazelden, 1995.

Fletcher, Anne M. *Sober for Good: New Solutions for Drinking Problems-Advice from Those Who Have Succeeded*. NY: Houghton Miflin Company, 2001.

Gilliam, Marianne W. *How Alcoholics Anonymous Failed Me*. NY: Eagle Brook, 1998.

Hemfelt, Robert and Fowler, Richard. *Serenity: A Companion for Twelve Step Recovery*. Nashville, TN: Thomas Nelson Publishers, 1990.

Jellinek, E. M. *The Disease Concept of Alcoholism*. New Haven, CN: College and University Press, 1960.

Johnson, Vernon E. *I'll Quit Tomorrow*. New York: Harper & Row, 1973.

K., Mitchell. *How It Worked: The Story of Clarence H. Snyder and The Early Days of Alcoholics Anonymous in Cleveland, Ohio*. NY: AA Big Book Study Group, 1997.

Ketcham, Katherine, and William F. Asbury (with Mel Schulstad and Arthur P. Ciaramicoli). *Beyond the Influence: Understanding and Defeating Alcoholism*. New York: Bantam Books, 2000.

Kavanaugh, Philip R. *Magnificent Addiction: Discovering Addiction as Gateway to Healing*. Santa Rosa, CA: Asland Publishing, 1992.

Kessel, Joseph. *The Road Back: A Report on Alcoholics Anonymous*. New York: Alfred A. Knopf, 1962.

Kurtz, Ernest and Ketcham, Katherine. *The Spirituality of Imperfection: Modern Wisdom from Classic Stories*. New York: Bantam Books, 1992.

Landry, Mim J. *Overview of Addiction Treatment Effectiveness*. Rev. ed., 1997. U.S. Department of Health and Human Services.

Larson, Joan Mathews. *Alcoholism-The Biochemical Connection: A Breakthrough Seven-Week Self-Treatment Program*. NY: Villard Books, 1992.

_____. *Seven Weeks to Sobriety: The Proven Program to Fight Alcoholism Through Nutrition*. New York: Fawcett Columbine, 1992

McCrady, Barbara S. and Miller, William R. *Research on Alcoholics Anonymous: Opportunities and* Alternatives. NJ: Publications Division, Rutgers Center of Alcohol Studies, 1993.

May, Gerald G. *Addiction & Grace: Love and Spirituality in the Healing of Addictions*. NY: HarperSanFrancisco, 1988.

McQ., Joe. *The Steps We Took*. Little Rock, AR: August House Publishers, Inc., 1990.

Miller, J. Keith. *A Hunger for Healing: The Twelve Steps as a Classic Model for Christian Spiritual Growth*. San Francisco: HarperSanFrancisco, 1991.

Nace, Edgar P. *The Treatment of Alcoholism*. NY: Brunner/Mazel Publishers, 1987.

O., Dr. Paul. *There's more to Quitting Drinking than Quitting Drinking.* Laguna Niguel, CA: Sabrina Publishing, 1995.

P., Wally. *Back to Basics: The Alcoholics Anonymous Beginners' Classes. Take all 12 Steps in Four One-Hour Sessions.* Tucson, AZ: Faith With Works Publishing Company, 1997.

Parham, A. Philip. *Letting God: Christian Meditations for Recovering Persons.* San Francisco: Harper & Row, 1987.

Peale, Norman Vincent. *The Positive Power of Jesus Christ: Life-Changing Adventures in Faith.* Pauling, NY: Foundation for Christian Living, 1980.

———. *The Power of Positive Thinking.* Pauling, NY: Peale Center for Christian Living, 1978.

Peele, Stanton. *Diseasing of America.* Lexington, MA Lexington Books, 1989.

_____. *The Truth About Addiction and Recovery* (with Archie Brodsky). MA: Lexington Books, 1995.

Poley, Wayne and Lea, Gary, and Vibe, Gail. *Alcoholism: A Treatment Manual.* NY: Gardner Press, Inc., 1979.

Playfair, William L. *The Useful Lie.* Wheaton, IL: Crossway Books, 1991.

Ragge, Ken. *More Revealed: A Critical Analysis of Alcoholics Anonymous and the Twelve Steps.* Henderson, NV: Alert! Publishing, 1991.

_____. *The Real AA: Behind the Myth of 12-Step Recovery.* AZ: Sharp Press, 1998.

Rudy, David R. *Becoming Alcoholic: Alcoholics Anonymous and the Reality of Alcoholism.* IL: Southern Illinois University Press, 1986.

Royce, James E. *Alcohol Problems and Alcoholism: A Comprehensive Survey.* NY: The Free Press, 1981.

Life Recovery Bible, The: The Living Bible. Wheaton, IL: Tyndale House Publishers, Inc., 1992.

Salomone, Guy. *Religious and Spiritual Origins of the Twelve Step Recovery Movement.* CA: Lotus Press, 1997.

Seiden, Jerry. *Divine or Distorted?: God As We Understand God.* San Diego, CA: Recovery Publications, 1993.

Selby, Saul. *Twelve Step Christianity: The Christian Roots & Application of the Twelve Steps.* MN: Hazelden, 2000.

Self-Help Sourcebook, The: Your Guide to Community and Online Support Groups. 6th.ed. compiled and edited by Barbara J. White and Edward J. Madara. Denville, NJ: American Self-Help Clearinghouse, 1994.

Shoemaker, Samuel M., Jr. *Revive Thy Church Beginning with Me.* New York: Harper & Brothers, 1948.

———. *The Church Alive.* New York: E. P. Dutton, 1951.

Spickard, Anderson and Thompson, Barbara R. *Dying for a Drink: What You Should Know about Alcoholism.* Waco, TX: Word Books Publisher, 1985.

Stafford, Tim. *The Hidden Gospel of the 12 Steps. Christianity Today*, July 22, 1991.

Trimpey, Jack. *Rational Recovery: The New Cure for Substance Addiction.* New York: Pocket Books, 1996.

———. *Revolutionary Alternative for Overcoming Alcohol and Drug Dependence, A: The Small Book.* Rev. ed. NY: Delacorte Press, 1992.

U.S. Department of Health and Human Services. Substance Abuse and Mental Health Services Administration. *National Household Survey on Drug Abuse: Main Findings 1996*. Rockville, MD: SAMHSA, Office of Applied Studies, 1998.

Vaillant, George E. *The Natural History of Alcoholism Revisited*. Cambridge, MA: Harvard University Press, 1995.

Van Impe, Jack and Campbell, Roger F. *Alcohol: The Beloved Enemy*. Nashville: Thomas Nelson Publishers, 1980.

Vaughan, Clark. *Addictive Thinking: The Road to Recovery for Problem Drinkers and Those Who Love Them*. NY: The Viking Press, 1982.

Wallis, Jim. *Faith Works. Lessons from the Life of an Activist Preacher*. NY: Random House, 2000.

W., Searcy. *A Study Book on my "Alcoholism Recovery" Since May 10, 1946 and a History of How Early A.A. Groups Started*. Revised. Dallas, TX: Searcy W., 1993.

Washton, Arnold and Boundy, Donna. *Willpower's Not Enough: Understanding and Recovering from Addictions of Every Kind*. NY: Harper & Row Publishers, 1989.

Way Home, The: A Spiritual Approach to Recovery. Orlando, FL: Bridge Builders, Inc., 1996.

White, William L. *Slaying The Dragon: The History of Addiction Treatment and Recovery in America*. Bloomington, IL: Chestnut Health Systems/Lighthouse Institute, 1998

Wing, Nell. *Grateful to have Been There: My 42 Years with Bill and Lois and the Evolution of Alcoholics Anonymous*. Park Ridge, IL: Parkside Publishing Corporation, 1992.

The Bible—Versions of and Books About

Authorized King James Version. New York: Thomas Nelson, 1984.

Benson, Clarence H. *A Popular History of Christian Education*. Chicago: Moody Press.

Bullinger, Ethelbert W. *A Critical Lexicon and Concordance to the English and Greek New Testament*. Michigan: Zondervan, 1981.

Burns, Kenneth Charles. "The Rhetoric of Christology." Master's thesis, San Francisco State University, 1991.

Every Catholic's Guide to the Sacred Scriptures. Nashville: Thomas Nelson, 1990.

Gray, James M. Synthetic Bible Studies: Containing an Outline Study of Every Book of the Bible, With Suggestions for Sermons, Addresses and Bible Expositions. New York: Fleming H. Revell Company.

Harnack, Adolph. *The Expansion of Christianity in the First Three Centuries*. New York: G. P. Putnam's Sons, Volume I, 1904; Volume II, 1905.

Jukes, Andrew. *The Names of GOD in Holy Scripture*. Michigan: Kregel Publications, 1967.

Kohlenberger, John R., III, gen. ed. *The Contemporary Parallel New Testament*. New York: Oxford University Press, 1997.

Mau, Charles P. *James M. Gray As a Christian Educator*. Master's thesis, Fuller Theological Seminary, 1963.

Megivern, James J. *Official Catholic Teachings: Bible Interpretation*. North Carolina: McGrath Publishing Company, 1978.

Moffatt, James. *A New Translation of the Bible*. New York: Harper & Brothers, 1954.

New Bible Dictionary. 2d ed. Wheaton, Illinois: Tyndale House Publishers, 1987.

On, J. Edwin. *Full Surrender*. London: Marshall, Morgan & Scott, 1951.

Phillips, J. B. *The New Testament in Modern English*. New York: The Macmillan Company, 1958.

Puskas, Charles B. *An Introduction to the New Testament*. Mass.: Hendrickson Publishers, 1989.

Recovery Devotional Bible. Grand Rapids, MI: Zondervan Publishing House, 1993.

Revised Standard Version. New York: Thomas Nelson, 1952.

Serenity: A Companion for Twelve Step Recovery. Nashville: Thomas Nelson, 1990.

Schaff, Philip. *History of the Christian Church*. Grand Rapids, MI: Wm. B. Eerdmans, Volume II, 1956.

Strong, James. *The Exhaustive Concordance of the Bible*. Iowa: Riverside Book and Bible House, n.d.

The Abingdon Bible Commentary. New York: Abingdon Press, 1929.

The Companion Bible. Michigan: Zondervan Bible Publishers, 1964.

The Life Recovery Bible. Wheaton, IL: Tyndale House Publishers, 1992.

The Revised English Bible. Oxford: Oxford University Press, 1989.

Vine, W. E. *Vine's Expository Dictionary of Old and New Testament Words*. New York: Fleming H. Revell, 1981.

Young's Analytical Concordance to the Bible. New York: Thomas Nelson, 1982.

Zodhiates, Spiros. *The Hebrew-Greek Key Study Bible*. 6th ed. AMG Publishers, 1991.

Bible Devotionals

Chambers, Oswald. *My Utmost for His Highest*. London: Simpkin Marshall, Ltd., 1927.

Clark, Glenn, *I Will Lift Up Mine Eyes*. New York: Harper & Brothers, 1937.

Dunnington, Lewis L. *Handles of Power*. New York: Abingdon-Cokesbury Press, 1942.

Fosdick, Harry Emerson. *The Meaning of Prayer*. New York: Association Press, 1915.

Holm, Nora Smith. *The Runner's Bible*. New York: Houghton Mifflin Company, 1915.

Jones, E. Stanley. *Abundant Living*. New York: Abingdon-Cokesbury Press, 1942.

———. *Victorious Living*. New York: Abingdon Press, 1936.

Parham, A. Philip. *Letting God: Christian Meditations for Recovering Persons*. New York: Harper & Row, 1987.

Prescott, D. M. *A New Day: Daily Readings for Our Time*. New ed. London: Grosvenor Books, 1979.

The Upper Room: Daily Devotions for Family and Individual Use. Quarterly. 1st issue: April, May, June, 1935. Edited by Grover Carlton Emmons. Nashville: General Committee on Evangelism through the Department of Home Missions, Evangelism, Hospitals, Board of Missions, Methodist Episcopal Church, South.

The Two Listeners. *God Calling*. Edited by A. J. Russell. Australia: DAYSTAR, 1953.

Tileston, Mary W. *Daily Strength for Daily Needs*. Boston: Roberts Brothers, 1893.

Publications by or about the Oxford Group & Oxford Group People

A Day in Pennsylvania Honoring Frank Nathan Daniel Buchman in Pennsburg and Allentown. Oregon: Grosvenor Books, 1992.

Allen, Geoffrey Francis. *He That Cometh*. New York: The Macmillan Company, 1933.

Almond, Harry J. *Foundations for Faith*. 2d ed. London: Grosvenor Books, 1980.

———. *Iraqi Statesman: A Portrait of Mohammed Fadhel Jamali*. Salem, OR: Grosvenor Books, 1993.

Austin, H. W. "Bunny". *Frank Buchman As I Knew Him*. London: Grosvenor Books, 1975.

———. *Moral Re-Armament: The Battle for Peace*. London: William Heinemann, 1938.

Batterson, John E. *How to Listen to God*. N.p., n.d.

Bayless, W. N. *The Oxford Group: A Way of Life*, n.d.

Becker, Mrs. George. "Quiet Time in the Home." N.p., n.d.

Begbie, Harold. *Life Changers*. New York: G. P. Putnam's Sons, 1927.

———. *Souls in Action*. New York: Hodder & Stoughton, 1911.

———. *Twice-Born Men*. New York: Fleming H. Revell, 1909.

Belden, David C. *The Origins and Development of the Oxford Group (Moral Re-Armament)*. D. Phil. Dissertation, Oxford University, 1976.

Belden, Kenneth D. *Beyond The Satellites: Is God is Speaking-Are We Listening?* London: Grosvenor Books, 1987.

———. *Meeting Moral Re-Armament*. London: Grosvenor Books, 1979.

———. *Reflections on Moral Re-Armament*. London: Grosvenor Books, 1983.

———. *The Hour of the Helicopter*. Somerset, England: Linden Hall, 1992.

Bennett, John C. *Social Salvation*. New York: Charles Scribner's Sons, 1935.

Benson, Clarence Irving. *The Eight Points of the Oxford Group*. London: Humphrey Milford, Oxford University Press, 1936.

Blair, David. *For Tomorrow-Yes!* Compiled and edited from David Blair's Notebook by Jane Mullen Blair & Friends. New York: Exposition Press, 1981.

Blair, Emily Newell. "The Oxford Group Challenges America." *Good Housekeeping*, October, 1936.

Blake, Howard C. *Way to Go: Adventures in Search of God's Will*. Burbank, CA: Pooh Stix Press, 1992.

Braden, Charles Samuel. *These Also Believe*. New York: The Macmillan Company, 1951.

Brown, Philip Marshall. *The Venture of Belief*. New York: Fleming H. Revell, 1935.

Buchman, Frank N. D. *Remaking the World*. London: Blandford Press, 1961.

———, and Sherwood Eddy. *Ten Suggestions for Personal Work* (not located).

———. *The Revolutionary Path: Moral Re-Armament in the thinking of Frank Buchman*. London: Grosvenor, 1975.

———. *Where Personal Work Begins*. Extracts and notes from talks given at the Lily Valley Conference near Kuling, China 1-13 August, 1918. London: Grosvenor Books, 1984.

Frank Buchman-80. Compiled by His Friends. London: Blandford Press, 1958.

Bundy, David D. *Keswick: A Bibliographic Introduction to the Higher Life Movements*. Wilmore, Kentucky: B. L. Fisher Library of Asbury Theological Seminary, 1975.

———. "Keswick and the Experience of Evangelical Piety." Chap. 7 in *Modern Christian Revivals*. Urbana, IL: University of Illinois Press, 1992.

Campbell, Paul. *The Art of Remaking Men*. Bombay: Himmat Publications, 1970.

———. *The Strategy of St. Paul*. London: Grosvenor Books, 1956.

———, and Peter Howard. *Remaking Men*. New York: Arrowhead Books, 1954.

Cantrill, Hadley. *The Psychology of Social Movements*. New York: John Wiley & Sons, Inc., 1941.

Carey, Walter, Bishop of Bloemfontein. *The Group System and the Catholic Church.* Archives of the Episcopal Church, Austin, Texas, n.d.

Chesteron, G. K. *The Well and The Shallows*, circa 1935, pp. 435-39.

Clapp, Charles, Jr. *The Big Bender.* New York: Harper & Row, 1938.

———. *Drinking's Not the Problem.* New York: Thomas Y. Crowell, 1949.

Clark, Walter Houston. *The Oxford Group: Its History and Significance.* New York: Bookman Associates, 1951.

Cook, Sydney and Garth Lean. *The Black and White Book: A Handbook of Revolution.* London: Blandford Press, 1972.

Crossman, R. H. S. *Oxford and the Groups.* Oxford: Basil Blackwell, 1934.

Crothers, Susan. *Susan and God.* New York: Harper & Brothers, 1939.

Day, Sherwood Sunderland. *The Principles of the Group.* Oxford: University Press, n.d.

Dayton, Donald W., ed. *The Higher Christian Life: Sources for the Study of the Holiness, Pentecostal and Keswick Movements.* New York: Garland Publishing, 1984.

Dinger, Clair M. *Moral Re-Armament: A Study of Its Technical and Religious Nature in the Light of Catholic Teaching.* Washington, D.C.: The Catholic University of America Press, 1961.

"Discord in Oxford Group: Buchmanites Ousted by Disciple from N.Y. Parish House." *Newsweek.* November 24, 1941.

Dorsey, Theodore H. *From a Far Country: The Conversion Story of a Campaigner for Christ.* Huntington, Indiana: Our Sunday Visitor Press, n.d.

Drakeford, John W. *People to People Therapy.* New York: Harper & Row, 1978.

Driberg, Tom. *The Mystery of Moral Re-Armament: A Study of Frank Buchman and His Movement.* New York: Alfred A. Knopf, 1965.

du Maurier, Daphne. *Come Wind, Come Weather.* London: William Heinemann, 1941.

Entwistle, Basil, and John McCook Roots. *Moral Re-Armament: What Is It?* Pace Publications, 1967.

Eister, Allan W. *Drawing Room Conversion.* Durham: Duke University Press, 1950.

Ferguson, Charles W. *The Confusion of Tongues.* Garden City: Doubleday, Doran Company, Inc., 1940.

Foot, Stephen. *Life Began Yesterday.* New York: Harper & Brothers, 1935.

Ford, John C., S.J. *Moral Re-Armament and Alcoholics Anonymous.* NCCA "Blue Book," Vol 10, 1968.

Forde, Eleanor Napier. *Guidance: What It Is and How to Get It.* Paper presented by Eleanor Napier Forde at Minnewaska, NY, September, 1927.

———. *The Guidance of God.* London: The Oxford Group, 1927.

Gordon, Anne Wolrige. *Peter Howard, Life and Letters.* London: Hodder & Stoughton, 1969.

Gray, Betty. *Watersheds: Journey to a faith.* London: Grosvenor, 1986.

Grensted, L. W. *The Person of Christ.* New York: Harper & Brothers, 1933.

Grogan, William. *John Riffe of the Steelworkers.* New York: Coward—McCann, 1959.

Hadden, Richard M. "Christ's Program for World-Reconstruction: Studies in the Sermon on the Mount." *The Calvary Evangel,* 1934-35, pp. 11-14, 44-49, 73-77, 104-07, 133-36.

Hamilton, A. S. Loudon. *MRA: How It All Began.* London: Moral Re-Armament, 1968.

———. *Some Basic Principles of Christian Work.* The Oxford Group, n.d.

————. "Description of the First Century Christian Fellowship." Vol. 2, *The Messenger*, June, 1923.

Hamlin, Bryan T. *Moral Re-Armament and Forgiveness in International Affairs*. London: Grosvenor, 1992.

Harris, Irving. *An Outline of the Life of Christ*. New York: The Oxford Group, 1935.

————. *Out in Front: Forerunners of Christ. A Study of the Lives of Eight Great Men*. New York: The Calvary Evangel, 1942.

————. *The Breeze of the Spirit*. New York: The Seabury Press, 1978.

Harrison, Marjorie. *Saints Run Mad*. London: John Lane, Ltd., 1934.

Henderson, Michael. *A Different Accent*. Richmond, VA: Grosvenor Books USA, 1985.

————. *All Her Paths Are Peace: Women Pioneers in Peacemaking*. CT: Kumerian Press, 1994.

————. *Hope for a Change: Commentaries by an Optimistic Realist*. Salem, OR: Grosvenor Books, 1991.

————. *On History's Coattails: Commentaries by an English Journalist in America*. Richmond, VA: Grosvenor USA, 1988.

Henson, Herbert Hensley. *The Oxford Group Movement*. London: Oxford University Press, 1933.

Hicks, Roger. *How Augustine Found Faith: Told in his own words from F. J. Sheed's translation of The Confessions of St. Augustine*. N.p., 1956.

————. *How to Read the Bible*. London: Moral Re-Armament, 1940.

————. *Letters to Parsi*. London: Blandford Press, 1960.

————. *The Endless Adventure*. London: Blandford Press, 1964.

————. *The Lord's Prayer and Modern Man*. London: Blandford Press, 1967.

Hofmeyr, Bremer. *How to Change*. New York: Moral Re-Armament, n.d.

————. *How to Listen*. London: The Oxford Group, 1941.

Holme, Reginald. *A Journalist for God: The memoirs of Reginald Holme*. London: A Bridge Builders Publication, 1995.

Holmes-Walker, Wilfrid. *The New Enlistment*. London: The Oxford Group, circa 1937.

Howard, Peter. *Frank Buchman's Secret*. Garden City: New York: Doubleday & Company, Inc., 1961.

————. *Fighters Ever*. London: William Heinemann, 1941

————. *Innocent Men*. London: William Heinemann, 1941.

————. *Ideas Have Legs*. London: Muller, 1945.

————. *That Man Frank Buchman*. London: Blandford Press, 1946.

————. *The World Rebuilt*. New York. Duell, Sloan & Pearce, 1951.

Hunter, T. Willard, with assistance from M.D.B. *A.A.'s Roots in the Oxford Group*. New York: A.A. Archives, 1988.

————. *Press Release*. Buchman Events/Pennsylvania, October 19, 1991.

————. *"It Started Right There" Behind the Twelve Steps and the Self-help Movement*. Oregon: Grosvenor Books, 1994.

————. *The Spirit of Charles Lindbergh: Another Dimension*. Lanham, MD: Madison Books, 1993.

————. *Uncommon Friends' Uncommon Friend*. A tribute to James Draper Newton, on the occasion of his eighty-fifth birthday. (Pamphlet, March 30, 1990).

————. *World Changing Through Life Changing*. Thesis, Newton Center, Mass: Andover-Newton Theological School, 1977.

Hutchinson, Michael. *A Christian Approach to Other Faiths*. London: Grosvenor Books, 1991.

———. *The Confessions*. (privately published study of St. Augustine's *Confessions*).

Jaeger, Clara. *Philadelphia Rebel: The Education of a Bourgeoise*. Virginia: Grosvenor, 1988.

Jones, Olive M. *Inspired Children*. New York: Harper & Brothers, 1933.

———. *Inspired Youth*. New York: Harper & Brothers, 1938.

Kitchen, V. C. *I Was a Pagan*. New York: Harper & Brothers, 1934.

Kestne, Eugene. *The Lord of History*. Boston: Daughters of St. Paul, 1980.

Koenig, His Eminence Franz Cardinal. *True Dialogue*. Oregon: Grosvenor USA, 1986.

Laun, Ferdinand. *Unter Gottes Fuhring*. The Oxford Group, n.d.

Lean, Garth. *Cast Out Your Nets*. London: Grosvenor, 1990.

———. *Frank Buchman: A Life*. London: Constable, 1985.

———. *Good God, It Works*. London: Blandford Press, 1974.

———. *Joyful Remembrance*. London: Executors of Garth D. Lean, 1994.

———. *On the Tail of a Comet: The Life of Frank Buchman*. Colorado Springs: Helmers & Howard, 1988.

———, and Morris Martin. *New Leadership*. London: William Heinemann, 1936.

Leon, Philip. A Philosopher's Quiet Time. N.p., n.d.

———. *The Philosophy of Courage or the Oxford Group Way*. New York: Oxford University Press, 1939.

"Less Buchmanism." *Time*, November 24, 1941.

Letter 7, The: The South African Adventure. A Miracle Working God Abroad. Oxford: The Groups, A First Century Christian Fellowship, 1930.

Macintosh, Douglas C. *Personal Religion*. New York: Charles Scribner's Sons, 1942.

Mackay, Malcom George. *More than Coincidence*. Edinburgh: The Saint Andrew Press, 1979.

Macmillan, Ebenezer. *Seeking and Finding*. New York: Harper & Brothers, 1933.

Margetson, The Very Reverend Provost. *The South African Adventure*. The Oxford Group, n.d.

Martin, Morris H. *Always a Little Further: Four Lives of a Luckie Felowe*. AZ: Elm Street Press, 2001.

_____.*The Thunder and the Sunshine*. Washington D.C.: MRA, n.d.

———. *Born to Live in the Future*. n.l.: Up With People, 1991.

McAll, Dr. Frances. *So what's the alternative?* London: Moral Re-Armament, 1974.

Molony, John N. *Moral Re-Armament*. Melbourne: The Australian Catholic Truth Society Record, June 10, 1956.

Mottu, Philippe. *The Story of Caux*. London: Grosvenor, 1970.

Mowat, R. C. *Modern Prophetic Voices: From Kierkegaard to Buchman*. Oxford: New Cherwel Press, 1994.

———. *The Message of Frank Buchman*. London: Blandford Press, n.d.

———. *Report on Moral Re-Armament*. London: Blandford Press, 1955.

———. *Creating the European Community*. London, 1973.

———. *Decline and Renewal: Europe Ancient and Modern*. Oxford: New Cherwel Press, 1991.

Moyes, John S. *American Journey*. Sydney: Clarendon Publishing Co., n. d.

Murray, Robert H. *Group Movements Throughout the Ages*. New York: Harper & Brothers. 1935.

Newton, Eleanor Forde. *I Always Wanted Adventure*. London: Grosvenor, 1992.

———. *Echoes From The Heart*. Fort Myers Beach, Florida, 1986.

Newton, James Draper. *Uncommon Friends: Life with Thomas Edison, Henry Ford, Harvey Firestone, Alexis Carrel, & Charles Lindbergh*. New York: Harcourt Brace, 1987.

Nichols, Beverley. *The Fool Hath Said*. Garden City: Doubleday, Doran & Company, 1936.

Orglmeister, Peter. *An Ideology for Today*. Pamphlet, 1965.

Perry, Edward T. *God Can Be Real*. Moral Re-Armament, Inc., 1969.

Petrocokino, Paul. *The New Man for the New World*. Cheshire: Paul Petrocokino, n.d.

———. *The Right Direction*. Great Britain: The City Press of Chester, Ltd., n.d.

———. *An Experiment: Try This For a Fortnight*. Privately published pamphlet, n.d.

Phillimore, Miles. *Just for Today*. Privately published pamphlet, 1940.

Prescott, D. M. *A New Day: Daily Readings for Our Time*. New ed. London: Grosvenor Book, 1979.

Raynor, Frank D., and Leslie D. Weatherhead. *The Finger of God*. London: Group Publications, Ltd., 1934.

Reynolds, Amelia S. *New Lives for Old*. New York. Fleming H. Revell, 1929.

Roots, The Right Reverend Herbert, Bishop of Hankow, China. *The Two Options*. The Oxford Group, 1934.

Roots, John McCook. *An Apostle to Youth*. Oxford, The Oxford Group, 1928.

Rose, Cecil. *When Man Listens*. New York: Oxford University Press, 1937.

Rose, Howard J. *The Quiet Time*. New York: Oxford Group at 61 Gramercy Park, North, 1937.

Russell, Arthur J. *For Sinners Only*. London: Hodder & Stoughton, 1932.

———. *One Thing I Know*. New York: Harper & Brothers, 1933.

Sangster, W. E. *God Does Guide Us*. New York: The Abingdon Press, 1934.

Sherry, Frank H. and Mahlon H. Hellerich. *The Formative Years of Frank N. D. Buchman*. (Reprint of article at Frank Buchman home in Allentown, Pennsylvania).

Spencer, F. A. M. *The Meaning of the Groups*. London: Methuen & Co., Ltd., 1934.

Spoerri, Theophil. *Dynamic out of Silence: Frank Buchman's Relevance Today*. Translated by John Morrison. London: Grosvenor Books, 1976.

Streeter, Burnett Hillman. *The God Who Speaks*. London: Macmillan & Co., Ltd., 1936.

———. *Reality*. London, 1943.

Suenens, Rt. Rev. Msgr. *The Right View of Moral Re-Armament*. London: Burns and Oates, 1952.

The Bishop of Leicester, Chancellor R. J. Campbell and the Editor of the "Church of England Newspaper." *Stories of our Oxford House Party.*, July 17, 1931.

The Groups in South Africa 1930. South Africa: The Groups, 1930.

The Layman with a Notebook. *What Is the Oxford Group?* London: Oxford University Press, 1933.

Thornhill, Alan. *One Fight More*. London: Frederick Muller, 1943.

———. *The Significance of the Life of Frank Buchman*. London: Moral Re-Armament, 1952.

———. *Best of Friends: A Life of Enriching Friendships*. United Kingdom, Marshall Pickering, 1986.

Thornton-Duesbury, Julian P. *Sharing*. The Oxford Group. n.d.

———. *The Oxford Group: A Brief Account of its Principles and Growth*. London: The Oxford Group, 1947.

———. *The Open Secret of MRA*. London: Blandford, 1964.

———. *A Visit to Caux: First-hand experience of Moral Re-Armament in action*. London: The Oxford Group, 1960.

"Calvary's Eviction of Buchman." *Time Magazine*, November 24, 1941.

Twitchell, Kenaston. *Do You Have to Be Selfish*. New York: Moral Re-Armament, n.d.

———. *How Do You Make Up Your Mind*. New York: Moral Re-Armament, n.d.

———. *Regeneration in the Ruhr*. Princeton: Princeton University Press, 1981.

———. *Supposing Your Were Absolutely Honest*. New York: Moral Re-Armament, n.d.

———. *The Strength of a Nation: Absolute Purity*. New York: Moral Re-Armament, n.d.

Van Dusen, Henry P. "Apostle to the Twentieth Century: Frank N. D. Buchman." *The Atlantic Monthly*, Vol. 154, pp. 1-16 (July 1934).

———. "The Oxford Group Movement: An Appraisal." *The Atlantic Monthly*. Vol. 154, pp. 230-252 (August 1934).

Viney, Hallen. *How Do I Begin?* The Oxford Group, 61 Gramercy Park, New York., 1937.

Vrooman, Lee. *The Faith That Built America*. New York: Arrowhead Books, Inc., 1955.

Waddy, Charis. *The Skills of Discernment*. London: Grosvenor Books, 1977.

Walter, Howard A. *Soul Surgery: Some Thoughts On Incisive Personal Work*. Oxford: The Oxford Group, 1928.

Watt, Frederick B. *Great Bear: A Journey Remembered*. Yellowknife, Northwest Territories, Canada: The Northern Publishers, 1980.

Weatherhead, Leslie D. *Discipleship*. London: Student Christian Movement Press, 1934.

———. *How Can I Find God?* London: Fleming H. Revell, 1934.

———. *Psychology and Life*. New York: Abingdon Press, 1935.

West, The Right Rev. George. *The World That Works*. London: Blandford, 1945.

Williamson, Geoffrey. *Inside Buchmanism*. New York: Philosophical Library, Inc., 1955.

Winslow, Jack C. *Church in Action* (no data available to author).

———. *Vital Touch with God: How to Carry on Adequate Devotional Life*. The Evangel, 8 East 40th St., New York, n.d.

———. *When I Awake*. London: Hodder & Stoughton, 1938.

———. *Why I Believe in the Oxford Group*. London: Hodder & Stoughton, 1934.

Books by or about Oxford Group Mentors

Bushnell, Horace. *The New Life*. London: Strahan & Co., 1868.

Chapman, J. Wilbur. *Life and Work of Dwight L. Moody*. Philadelphia, 1900.

Cheney, Mary B. *Life and Letters of Horace Bushnell*. New York: Harper & Brothers, 1890.

Drummond, Henry. *Essays and Addresses*. New York: James Potts & Company, 1904.

———. *Natural Law in the Spiritual World*. Potts Edition.

———. *The Changed Life*. New York: James Potts & Company, 1891.

———. *The Greatest Thing in the World and Other Addresses*. London: Collins, 1953.

————. *The Ideal Life*. London: Hodder & Stoughton, 1897.

————. *The New Evangelism and Other Papers*. London: Hodder & Stoughton, 1899.

Edwards, Robert L. *Of Singular Genius, of Singular Grace: A Biography of Horace Bushnell*. Cleveland: The Pilgrim Press, 1992.

Findlay, James F., Jr. *Dwight L. Moody American Evangelist*. Chicago, University of Chicago Press, 1969.

Fitt, Emma Moody, *Day by Day with D. L. Moody*. Chicago: Moody Press, n.d.

Goodspeed, Edgar J. *The Wonderful Career of Moody and Sankey in Great Britain and America*. New York: Henry S. Goodspeed & Co., 1876.

Guldseth, Mark O. *Streams*. Alaska: Fritz Creek Studios, 1982.

Hopkins, C. Howard. *John R. Mott, a Biography*. Grand Rapids: William B. Erdmans Publishing Company, 1979.

James, William. *The Varieties of Religious Experience*. New York: First Vintage Books/The Library of America, 1990.

Meyer, F. B. *Five Musts*. Chicago: Moody Press, 1927.

————. *The Secret of Guidance*. New York: Fleming H. Revell, 1896.

Moody, Paul D. *My Father: An Intimate Portrait of Dwight Moody*. Boston: Little Brown, 1938.

Moody, William R. *The Life of D. L. Moody*. New York: Fleming H. Revell, 1900.

Mott, John R. *The Evangelization of the World in This Generation*. London, 1901.

————. *Addresses and Papers* (no further data at this time).

————. *Five Decades and a Forward View*. 4th ed. New York: Harper & Brothers, 1939.

Pollock, J. C. *Moody: A Biographical Portrait of the Pacesetter in Modern Mass Evangelism*. New York: Macmillan, 1963.

Smith, George Adam. *The Life of Henry Drummond*. New York: McClure, Phillips & Co., 1901.

Speer, Robert E. *Studies of the Man Christ Jesus*. New York: Fleming H. Revell, 1896.

————. *The Marks of a Man*. New York: Hodder & Stoughton, 1907.

————. *The Principles of Jesus*. New York: Fleming H. Revell Company, 1902.

Stewart, George, Jr. *Life of Henry B. Wright*. New York: Association Press, 1925.

Wright, Henry B. *The Will of God and a Man's Lifework*. New York: The Young Men's Christian Association Press, 1909.

Publications by or about Samuel Moor Shoemaker, Jr.

Shoemaker, Samuel Moor, Jr., "A 'Christian Program.'" In *Groups That Work: The Key to Renewal . . . for Churches, Communities, and Individuals*. Compiled by Walden Howard and the Editors of Faith At Work. Michigan: Zondervan, 1967.

————. "Act As If." *Christian Herald*. October, 1954.

————. "A First Century Christian Fellowship: A Defense of So-called Buchmanism by One of Its Leaders." Reprinted from the *Churchman*, circa 1928.

————. "And So from My Heart I Say . . ." *The A.A. Grapevine*. New York: The A.A. Grapevine, Inc., September, 1948.

————. *. . . And Thy Neighbor*. Waco, Texas: Word Books, 1967.

————. *A Young Man's View of the Ministry*. New York: Association Press, 1923.

————. *Beginning Your Ministry*. New York: Harper & Row Publishers, 1963.

————. *By the Power of God*. New York: Harper & Brothers, 1954.

———. *Calvary Church Yesterday and Today*. New York: Fleming H. Revell, 1936.

———. *Children of the Second Birth*. New York: Fleming H. Revell, 1927.

———. *Christ and This Crisis*. New York: Fleming H. Revell, 1943.

———. *Christ's Words from the Cross*. New York: Fleming H. Revell, 1933.

———. *Confident Faith*. New York: Fleming H. Revell, 1932.

———. *Extraordinary Living for Ordinary Men*. Michigan: Zondervan, 1965.

———. *Faith at Work*. A symposium edited by Samuel Moor Shoemaker. Hawthorne Books, 1958.

———. *Freedom and Faith*. New York: Fleming H. Revell, 1949.

———. *God and America*. New York: Book Stall, 61 Gramercy Park North, New York, n.d.

———. *God's Control*. New York: Fleming H. Revell, 1939.

———. *How to Become a Christian*. New York: Harper & Brothers, 1953.

———. "How to Find God." *The Calvary Evangel*. July, 1957, pp. 1-24.

———. *How to Help People*. Cincinnati: Forward Movement Publications, 1976.

———. *How You Can Find Happiness*. New York: E. P. Dutton & Co., 1947.

———. *How You Can Help Other People*. New York: E. P. Dutton & Co., 1946.

———. *If I Be Lifted Up*. New York: Fleming H. Revell, 1931.

———. *In Memoriam: The Service of Remembrance*. Princeton: The Graduate Council, Princeton University, June 10, 1956.

———. *Living Your Life Today*. New York: Fleming H. Revell, 1947.

———. "Lord, Teach Us to Pray." *Creative Help for Daily Living* (Foundation for Christian Living, Pawling, New York) 28, no. 2 (1977), Part ii.

———. *Morning Radio Talk No. 1, by Reverend Samuel M. Shoemaker*, American Broadcasting Co., 1 page transcript of program for October 4, 1945.

———. *My Life-Work and My Will*. Pamphlet, Christian ministry conference, Concord, N.H., circa 1930.

———. *National Awakening*. New York: Harper & Brothers, 1936.

———. *One Boy's Influence*. New York: Association Press, 1925.

———. *Realizing Religion*. New York: Association Press, 1923.

———. *Religion That Works*. New York: Fleming H. Revell, 1928.

———. *Revive Thy Church*. New York: Harper & Brothers, 1948.

———. *Sam Shoemaker at His Best*. New York: Faith At Work, 1964.

———. *So I Stand by the Door and Other Verses*. Pittsburgh: Calvary Rectory, 1958.

———. *Steps of a Modern Disciple*. Atlanta, GA: Lay Renewal Publications, 1972.

———. *The Breadth and Narrowness of the Gospel*. New York: Fleming H. Revell, 1929.

———. *The Calvary Evangel, monthly articles in*. New York. Calvary Episcopal Church.

———. *The Church Alive*. New York: E. P. Dutton & Co., Inc., 1951.

———. *The Church Can Save the World*. New York: Harper & Brothers, 1938.

———. *The Conversion of the Church*. New York: Fleming H. Revell, 1932.

———. "The Crisis of Self-Surrender." *Guideposts*. November, 1955.

———. *The Experiment of Faith*. New York: Harper & Brothers. 1957.

———. *The Gospel According to You*. New York: Fleming H. Revell, 1934.

———. *The James Houston Eccleston Day-Book: Containing a Short Account of His Life and Readings for Every Day in the Year Chosen from His Sermons*. Compiled by Samuel M. Shoemaker, Jr. New York: Longmans, Green & Co., 1915.

———. "The Spiritual Angle." *The A.A. Grapevine*. New York: The A.A. Grapevine, Inc., October, 1955.

———. "The Way to Find God." *The Calvary Evangel* (August, 1935).

———. *They're on the Way*. New York: E. P. Dutton, 1951.

———. "Creative Relationships." In *Together*. New York: Abingdon Cokesbury Press, 1946.

———. "The Twelve Steps of A.A.: What They Can Mean to the Rest of Us." *The Calvary Evangel*. New York: The Evangel, 1953.

———. "Those Twelve Steps As I Understand Them." *Best of the Grapevine: Volume II*. New York: The A.A. Grapevine, Inc., 1986.

———. "12 Steps to Power." *Faith At Work News*. Reprint. 1983.

———. *Twice-Born Ministers*. New York: Fleming H. Revell, 1929.

———. *Under New Management*. Grand Rapids: Zondervan Publishing House., 1966.

———. *What the Church Has to Learn from Alcoholics Anonymous*. Reprint of 1956 sermon. Available at A.A. Archives, New York.

———. *With the Holy Spirit and with Fire*. New York: Harper & Brothers, 1960.

A Guide to Calvary Episcopal Church: 125th Anniversary 1855-1980. Pittsburgh: Calvary Episcopal Church, 1980.

"Buchman Religion Explained to 1,000." *New York Times*. May 27, 1931.

"Calvary Mission." Pamphlet. New York: Calvary Episcopal Church, n.d.

"Campus Calls by Dr. Shoemaker Foster Chain of Religious Cells." *New York Tribune*. February 25, 1951.

Centennial History: Calvary Episcopal Church, 1855-1955. Pittsburgh: Calvary Episcopal Church, 1955.

"Church Ejects Buchman Group." *New York Times*. November 8, 1941.

"Crusaders of Reform." *Princeton Alumni Weekly*. June 2, 1993.

Cuyler, John Potter, Jr. *Calvary Church in Action*. New York: Fleming H. Revell, 1934.

Day, Sherwood S. "Always Ready: S.M.S. As a Friend." *The Evangel* (New York: Calvary Church, July-August, 1950).

Get Changed; Get Together; Get Going: A History of the Pittsburgh Experiment. Pittsburgh: The Pittsburgh Experiment, n.d.

Harris, Irving. *The Breeze of the Spirit*. New York: The Seabury Press, 1978.

———. "S.M.S.—Man of God for Our Time." *Faith At Work* (January-February, 1964).

"Houseparties Across the Continent." *The Christian Century*. August 23, 1933.

Knippel, Charles Taylor. *Samuel M. Shoemaker's Theological Influence on William G. Wilson's Twelve Step Spiritual Program of Recovery (Alcoholics Anonymous)*. Dissertation. St. Louis University, 1987.

"Listening to God Held Daily Need." *New York Times*. December 4, 1939.

Norton-Taylor, Duncan. "Businessmen on Their Knees." *Fortune*. October, 1953.

Olsson, Karl A. "The History of Faith at Work" (five parts). *Faith at Work News*. 1982-1983.

Peale, Norman Vincent. "The Unforgettable Sam Shoemaker." *Faith At Work*. January, 1964.

———. "The Human Touch: The Estimate of a Fellow Clergyman and Personal Friend." *The Evangel* (New York: Calvary Church, July-August, 1950).

Pitt, Louis W. "New Life, New Reality: A Brief Picture of S.M.S.'s Influence in the Diocese of New York." *Faith at Work*, July-August, 1950.

"Pittsburgh Man of the Year." *Pittsburgh Post Gazette*. January 12, 1956.

Sack, David Edward. *Sam Shoemaker and the "Happy Ethical Pagans."* Princeton, New Jersey: paper prepared in the Department of Religion, Princeton University, June, 1993.

"Sam Shoemaker and Faith at Work." Pamphlet on file at Faith At Work, Inc., 150 S. Washington St., Suite 204, Falls Church, VA 22046.

Schwartz, Robert. "Laymen and Clergy to Join Salute to Dr. S. M. Shoemaker." *Pittsburgh Press*. December 10, 1961.

Shoemaker, Helen Smith. *I Stand by the Door*. New York: Harper & Row, 1967.

"Sees Great Revival Near." *New York Times*. September 8, 1930.

Sider, Michael J. *Taking the Gospel to the Point: Evangelicals in Pittsburgh and the Origins of the Pittsburgh Leadership Foundation*. Pittsburgh: Pittsburgh Leadership Foundation, n.d.

"Soul Clinic Depicted By Pastor in Book." *New York Times*. August 5, 1927.

"Ten of the Greatest American Preachers." *Newsweek*. March 28, 1955.

The Pittsburgh Experiment's Groups. Pittsburgh: The Pittsburgh Experiment, n.d.

Tools for Christian Living. Pittsburgh: The Pittsburgh Experiment, n.d.

"Urges Church Aid Oxford Group." *New York Times*. January 2, 1933, p. 26.

Wilson, Bill. "I Stand by the Door." *The A.A. Grapevine*. New York: The A.A. Grapevine, Inc., February, 1967.

Woolverton, John F. "Evangelical Protestantism and Alcoholism 1933-1962: Episcopalian Samuel Shoemaker, The Oxford Group and Alcoholics Anonymous." *Historical Magazine of the Protestant Episcopal Church* 52 (March, 1983).

[The reader may find additional material by or about Samuel Shoemaker, Jr., at: (1) the Maryland Historical Society, Manuscripts Division, under "Shoemaker Papers;" (2) the Princeton University Archives at Princeton University, Olden Lane, Princeton, New Jersey, in the Samuel Shoemaker alumnus file; (3) the Episcopal Church Archives in Austin, Texas; (4) the Library of Congress, in the Ray Foote Purdy files of the Moral Re-Armament (and Oxford Group) Archives; (5) the Maryland Diocese of the Protestant Episcopal Church; (6) the Stepping Stones Archives, Bedford Hills, New York, the Shoemaker-Wilson letters; (7) the Hartford Theological Seminary Archives, Hartford, Connecticut; and (8) the parish offices of Calvary/St. George's in New York City. In addition, articles by or about Shoemaker were written in *The Calvary Evangel*, published by Calvary Episcopal Church in New York; in the *Faith at Work* magazine, 150 South Washington Street, Suite 204, Falls Church, Virginia; and in the literature of The Pittsburgh Experiment, 1802 Investment Building, Pittsburgh, Pennsylvania 15222.]

Spiritual Literature-Non-Oxford Group

[Almost all of these books were owned, studied, recommended, and loaned to others by Dr. Bob and his wife, Anne.]

Allen, James. *As a Man Thinketh*. New York: Peter Pauper Press, n.d.

———. *Heavenly Life*. New York: Grosset & Dunlap, n.d.

Barton, George A. *Jesus of Nazareth*. New York: The Macmillan Company, 1922.

Bode, Carl, ed. *The Portable Emerson*. New ed. New York: Penguin Books, 1981.

Brother Lawrence. *The Practice of the Presence of God*. Pennsylvania: Whitaker House, 1982.

Browne, Lewis. *This Believing World: A Simple Account of the Great Religions of Mankind*. New York: The Macmillan Co., 1935.

Carruthers, Donald W. *How to Find Reality in Your Morning Devotions*. Pennsylvania: State College, n.d.

Chambers, Oswald. *Studies in the Sermon on the Mount*. London: Simpkin, Marshall, Ltd., n.d.

Clark, Francis E. *Christian Endeavor in All Lands*. N.p.: The United Society of Christian Endeavor, 1906.

Clark, Glenn. *Clear Horizons*. Vol 2. Minnesota: Macalester Park Publishing, 1941.

———. *Fishers of Men*. Boston: Little, Brown, 1928.

———. *God's Reach*. Minnesota: Macalester Park Publishing, 1951.

———. *How to Find Health through Prayer*. New York: Harper & Brothers, 1940.

———. *I Will Lift Up Mine Eyes*. New York: Harper & Brothers, 1937.

———. *Stepping Heavenward: The Spiritual Journal of Louise Miles Clark*. Minnesota: Macalester Park Publishing, 1940.

———. *The Lord's Prayer and Other Talks on Prayer from The Camps Farthest Out*. Minnesota: Macalester Publishing Co., 1932.

———. *The Man Who Talks with Flowers*. Minnesota: Macalester Park Publishing, 1939.

———. *The Soul's Sincere Desire*. Boston: Little, Brown, 1925.

———. *Touchdowns for the Lord. The Story of "Dad" A. J. Elliott*. Minnesota: Macalester Park Publishing Co., 1947.

———. *Two or Three Gathered Together*. New York: Harper & Brothers, 1942.

Daily, Starr. *Recovery*. Minnesota: Macalester Park Publishing, 1948.

Eddy, Mary Baker. *Science and Health with Key to the Scriptures*. Boston: Published by the Trustees under the Will of Mary Baker G. Eddy, 1916.

Fillmore, Charles. *Christian Healing*. Kansas City: Unity School of Christianity, 1936.

———, and Cora Fillmore. *Teach Us To Pray*. Lee's Summit, Missouri: Unity School of Christianity, 1950.

Fosdick, Harry Emerson. *A Great Time to Be Alive*. New York: Harper & Brothers, 1944.

———. *As I See Religion*. New York: Grosset & Dunlap, 1932.

———. *On Being a Real Person*. New York: Harper & Brothers, 1943.

———. *The Man from Nazareth*. New York: Harper & Brothers, 1949.

———. *The Manhood of the Master*. London: Student Christian Association, 1924.

———. *The Meaning of Faith*. New York: The Abingdon Press, 1917.

———. *The Meaning of Prayer*. New York: Association Press, 1915.

———. *The Meaning of Service*. London: Student Christian Movement, 1921.

Fox, Emmet. *Alter Your Life*. New York: Harper & Brothers, 1950.

———. *Find and Use Your Inner Power*. New York: Harper & Brothers, 1937.

———. *Power through Constructive Thinking*. New York: Harper & Brothers, 1932.

———. *Sparks of Truth*. New York: Grosset & Dunlap, 1941.

———. *The Sermon on the Mount*. New York: Harper & Row, 1934.

———. Pamphlets: *Getting Results by Prayer* (1933); *The Great Adventure* (1937); *You Must Be Born Again* (1936).

Glover, T. R. *The Jesus of History*. New York: Association Press, 1930.

Gordon, S. D. *The Quiet Time*. London: Fleming, n.d.

Graeser, Mark H., Lynn, John A., Schoenheit, John W. *Don't Blame God: A Biblical Answer to the Problem of Evil, Sin and Suffering*, 4th ed. Indiana: Christian Educational Services, 1994

Heard, Gerald. *A Preface to Prayer*. New York: Harper & Brothers, 1944.

Herman, E. *Creative Prayer*. London: James Clarke & Co., circa 1921.

Hickson, James Moore. *Heal the Sick*. London: Methuen & Co., 1925.

James, William. *The Varieties of Religious Experience*. New York: First Vintage Press/The Library of America Edition, 1990.

Jones, E. Stanley. *Abundant Living*. New York: Cokesbury Press, 1942.

————. *Along the Indian Road*. New York: Abingdon Press, 1939.

————. *Christ and Human Suffering*. New York: Abingdon Press, 1930.

————. *Christ at the Round Table*. New York: Abingdon Press, 1928.

————. *The Choice Before Us*. New York: Abingdon Press, 1937.

————. *The Christ of Every Road*. New York: Abingdon Press, 1930.

————. *The Christ of the American Road*. New York: Abingdon-Cokesbury Press, 1944.

————. *The Christ of the Indian Road*. New York: Abingdon Press, 1925.

————. *The Christ of the Mount*. New York: Abingdon Press, 1930.

————. *Victorious Living*. New York: Abingdon Press, 1936.

————. *Way to Power and Poise*. New York: Abingdon Press, 1949.

Jung, Dr. Carl G. *Modern Man in Search of a Soul*. New York: Harcourt Brace Jovanovich, 1933.

Kagawa, Toyohiko. *Love: The Law of Life*. Philadelphia: The John C. Winston Company, 1929.

Kempis, Thomas à. *The Imitation of Christ*. Georgia: Mercer University Press, 1989.

Kenyon, E. W. *In His Presence*. Kenyon's Gospel Publishing Society, Inc., 1999.

_____. *Jesus the Healer*. Kenyon's Gospel Publishing Society, 2000.

_____. *The Hidden Man*. WA: Kenyon's Gospel Publishing Society, Inc., 1998.

_____. *The Wonderful Name of Jesus*. Kenyon's Gospel Publishing Society, 1998.

Laubach, Frank. *Prayer (Mightiest Force in the World)*. New York: Fleming H. Revell, 1946.

Laymon, Charles M. *A Primer of Prayer*. Nashville: Tidings, 1949.

Lieb, Frederick G. *Sight Unseen*. New York: Harper & Brothers, 1939.

Ligon, Ernest M. *Psychology of a Christian Personality*. New York: Macmillan, 1935.

Link, Dr. Henry C. *The Rediscovery of Man*. New York: Macmillan, 1939.

Lupton, Dilworth. *Religion Says You Can*. Boston: The Beacon Press, 1938.

Moseley, J. Rufus. *Perfect Everything*. Minnesota: Macalester Publishing Co., 1949.

Oursler, Fulton. *Happy Grotto*. Declan and McMullen, 1948.

————. *The Greatest Story Ever Told*. New York: Doubleday, 1949.

Parker, William R., and Elaine St. Johns. *Prayer Can Change Your Life*. New ed. New York: Prentice Hall, 1957.

Peale, Norman Vincent. *The Art of Living*. New York: Abingdon-Cokesbury Press, 1937.

Rawson, F. L. *The Nature of True Prayer*. Chicago: The Marlowe Company, n.d.

Sheean, Vincent. *Lead Kindly Light*. New York: Random House, 1949.

Sheen, Fulton J. *Peace of Soul*. New York: McGraw Hill, 1949.

Sheldon, Charles M. *In His Steps*. Nashville, Broadman Press, 1935.

Silkey, Charles Whitney. *Jesus and Our Generation*. Chicago: University of Chicago Press, 1925.

Speer, Robert E.. *Studies of the Man Christ Jesus*. New York: Fleming H. Revell, 1896.

Stalker, James. *The Life of Jesus Christ*. New York: Fleming H. Revell, 1891.

The Confessions of St. Augustine. Translated by E. B. Pusey. A Cardinal Edition. New York: Pocket Books, 1952.

The Fathers of the Church. New York: CIMA Publishing, 1947.

Trine, Ralph Waldo. *In Tune with the Infinite*. New York: Thomas H. Crowell, 1897.

———. *The Man Who Knew*. New York: Bobbs Merrill, 1936.

Troward, Thomas. *The Edinburgh Lectures on Mental Science*. N.p., n.d.

Uspenskii, Peter D. *Tertium Organum*. New York: A.A. Knopf, 1922.

Weatherhead, Leslie D. *Discipleship*. New York: Abingdon Press, 1934.

———. *How Can I Find God?* New York: Fleming H. Revell, 1934.

———. *Psychology and Life*. New York: Abingdon Press, 1935.

Wells, Amos R. *Expert Endeavor: A Text-book of Christian Endeavor Methods and Principles*. Boston: United Society of Christian Endeavor, 1911.

Werber, Eva Bell. *Quiet Talks with the Master*. L.A.: De Vorss & Co., 1942.

Williams, R. Llewelen, *God's Great Plan, a Guide to the Bible*. Hoverhill Destiny Publishers, n.d.

Willitts, Ethel R. *Healing in Jesus Name*. Chicago: Ethel R. Willitts Evangelists, 1931.

Worcester, Elwood, Samuel McComb, and Isador H. Coriat. *Religion and Medicine: The Moral Control of Nervous Disorders*. New York: Moffat, Yard & Company, 1908.

Yancey, Philip. *Soul Survivor: How My Faith Survived the Church*. NY: Doubleday, 2001.

Dick B.'s Historical Titles on Early A.A.'s Spiritual Roots and Successes

Dr. Bob and His Library: A Major A.A. Spiritual Source (3rd Edition)
　　Fwd. by Ernest Kurtz, Ph.D., Author, *Not-God: A History of Alcoholics Anonymous.*
A study of the immense spiritual reading of the Bible, Christian literature, and Oxford Group books done and recommended by A.A. co-founder, Dr. Robert H. Smith. Paradise Research Pub., Inc.; 156 pp.; 6 x 9; perfect bound; $15.95; 1998; ISBN 1-885803-25-7.

Anne Smith's Journal, 1933-1939 (3rd Edition)
　　Fwd. by Robert R. Smith, son of Dr. Bob & Anne; co-author, *Children of the Healer.*
Dr. Bob's wife, Anne, kept a journal in the 1930's from which she shared with early AAs and their families ideas from the Bible and the Oxford Group. Her ideas substantially influenced A.A.'s program. Paradise Research Publications, 180 pp.; 6 x 9; perfect bound; 1998; $16.95; ISBN 1-885803-24-9.

The Oxford Group & Alcoholics Anonymous (Second Edition)
　　Foreword by Rev. T. Willard Hunter; author, columnist, Oxford Group activist.
A comprehensive history of the origins, principles, practices, and contributions to A.A. of "A First Century Christian Fellowship" (also known as the Oxford Group) of which A.A. was an integral part in the developmental period between 1931 and 1939. Paradise Research Publications; 432 pp.; 6 x 9; perfect bound; 1998; $17.95; ISBN 1-885803-19-2. (Previous title: *Design for Living*).

The Akron Genesis of Alcoholics Anonymous (Newton Edition)
　　Foreword by former U.S. Congressman John F. Seiberling of Akron, Ohio.
The story of A.A.'s birth at Dr. Bob's Home in Akron on June 10, 1935. Tells what early AAs did in their meetings, homes, and hospital visits; what they read; how their ideas developed from the Bible, Oxford Group, and Christian literature. Depicts roles of A.A. founders and their wives; Henrietta Seiberling; and T. Henry Williams. Paradise Research Publications; 400 pp., 6 x 9; perfect bound; 1998; $17.95; ISBN 1-885803-17-6.

The Books Early AAs Read for Spiritual Growth (7th Edition)
　　Foreword by former U.S. Congressman John F. Seiberling of Akron, Ohio.
The most exhaustive bibliography (with brief summaries) of all the books known to have been read and recommended for spiritual growth by early AAs in Akron and on the East Coast. Paradise Research Publications; 126 pp.; 6 x 9; perfect bound; 1998; $15.95; ISBN 1-885803-26-5.

New Light on Alcoholism: God, Sam Shoemaker, and A.A. (Second Edition)
　　Forewords by Nickie Shoemaker Haggart, daughter of Sam Shoemaker; Julia Harris; and Karen Plavan, Ph.D.
A comprehensive history and analysis of the all-but-forgotten specific contributions to A.A. spiritual principles and practices by New York's famous Episcopal preacher, the Rev. Dr. Samuel M. Shoemaker, Jr.—dubbed by Bill W. a "co-founder" of A.A. and credited by Bill as the well-spring of A.A.'s spiritual recovery ideas. Paradise Research Pub.; approx. 672 pp.; 6 x 9; perfect bound; 1999; $24.95; ISBN 1-885803-27-3.

The Good Book and The Big Book: A.A.'s Roots in the Bible (Second Edition)
　　Fwd. by Robert R. Smith, son of Dr. Bob & Anne; co-author, *Children of the Healer*.
The author shows conclusively that A.A.'s program of recovery came primarily from the Bible. This is a history of A.A.'s biblical roots as they can be seen in A.A.'s Big Book, Twelve Steps, and Fellowship. Paradise Research Publications; 264 pp.; 6 x 9; perfect bound; 1997; $17.95; ISBN 1-885803-16-8.

That Amazing Grace: The Role of Clarence and Grace S. in Alcoholics Anonymous
　　Foreword by Harold E. Hughes, former U.S. Senator from, and Governor of, Iowa.

Precise details of early A.A.'s spiritual practices—from the recollections of Grace S., widow of A.A. pioneer, Clarence S. Paradise Research Pub.; 160 pp.; 6 x 9; perfect bound; 1996; $16.95; ISBN 1-885803-06-0.

Good Morning!: Quiet Time, Morning Watch, Meditation, and Early A.A. (2d Ed.) A practical guide to Quiet Time—considered a "must" in early A.A. Also discusses biblical roots, history, helpful books, and how to. Paradise Research Pub.; 154 pp.; 6 x 9; perfect bound; 1998; $16.95; ISBN: 1-885803-22-2.

Turning Point: A History of Early A.A.'s Spiritual Roots and Successes
Fwd. by Paul Wood, Ph.D., Pres., Nat. Council on Alcoholism and Drug Dependence. *Turning Point* is a comprehensive history of early A.A.'s spiritual roots and successes. It is the culmination of six years of research, traveling, and interviews. Dick B.'s latest title shows specifically what the Twelve Step pioneers borrowed from: (1) The Bible; (2) The Rev. Sam Shoemaker's teachings; (3) The Oxford Group; (4) Anne Smith's Journal; and (5) meditation periodicals and books, such as *The Upper Room*. Paradise Research Publications; 776 pp.; 6 x 9; perfect bound; 1997; $29.95; ISBN: 1-885803-07-9.

Utilizing Early A.A.'s Spiritual Roots for Recovery Today
This booklet is the first of a series containing the remarks of Dick B. at his annual seminars at The Wilson House—birthplace of A.A. co-founder Bill Wilson. It is intended as a guide for study groups who wish to apply today the highly successful program and principles of early A.A.. Paradise Research Publications; 106 pp.; 6 x 9; perfect bound; 2000; $14.95; ISBN 1-885803-28-1.

The Golden Text of A.A.: God, the Pioneers, and Real Spirituality
This booklet is the second of a series containing the remarks of Dick B. at his annual seminars at The Wilson House. The booklet contains the sincere and surprising credit that Bill Wilson and Bill Dotson (A.A. #3) gave to God for curing them of the disease of alcoholism; Paradise Research Publications; 94pp; 6 x 9; perfect bound; 2000; $14.95; ISBN 1-885803-29-X.

By the Power of God: A Guide to Early A.A. Groups & Forming Similar Groups Today
Fwd. by Ozzie Lepper, Pres./Managing Dir., The Wilson House, East Dorset, VT. Precise details of early A.A.'s spiritual practices—from the recollections of Grace S., widow of A.A. pioneer, Clarence S. Paradise Research Pub.; 260 pp.; 6 x 9; perfect bound; 2000; $16.95; ISBN 1-885803-30-3.

Why Early A.A. Succeeded: The Good Book in Alcoholics Anonymous Yesterday and Today
Foreword by Jeffrey H. Boyd, M.D., M. Div., M.P.H.; Chairman of Psychiatry, Waterbury Hospital, Waterbury, CT; Ordained Episcopal Minister; Chairman of the New England Evangelical Theological Society.
Paradise Research Pub.; approx 330 pp.; 6 x 9; perfect bound; 2001; $17.95; ISBN 1-885803-31-1.

Making Known the Biblical History and Roots of Alcoholics Anonymous: An Eleven-Year Research, Writing, Publishing, and Fact Dissemination Project
A detailed bibliography and inventory of more than 23,900 historical books, articles, pamphlets, papers, videos, audio tapes, news clippings, and other archival materials accumulated in the past eleven years and used in the research and publication of Dick B.'s 18 published titles on A.A.'s history and biblical roots.
Paradise Research Publications, Inc.; 153 pp.; 8 1/2 x 11; spiral bound; 2001; $24.95; ISBN: 1-885803-32-X.

About the Author

Dick B. writes books on the spiritual roots of Alcoholics Anonymous. They show how the basic and highly successful biblical ideas used by early AAs can be valuable tools for success in today's A.A. His research can also help the religious and recovery communities work more effectively with alcoholics, addicts, and others involved in Twelve Step programs.

The author is an active, recovered member of A.A.; a retired attorney; and a Bible student. He has sponsored more than eighty men in their recovery from alcoholism. Consistent with A.A.'s traditions of anonymity, he uses the pseudonym "Dick B."

He has had fifteen titles published: *Dr. Bob and His Library*; *Anne Smith's Journal, 1933-1939*; *The Oxford Group & Alcoholics Anonymous: A Design for Living That Works*; *The Akron Genesis of Alcoholics Anonymous*; *The Books Early AAs Read for Spiritual Growth*; *New Light on Alcoholism: God, Sam Shoemaker, and A.A.*; *Courage to Change* (with Bill Pittman); *The Good Book and The Big Book: A.A.'s Roots in the Bible*; *That Amazing Grace: The Role of Clarence and Grace S. in Alcoholics Anonymous*; *Good Morning!: Quiet Time, Morning Watch, Meditation, and Early A.A.*; *Turning Point: A History of Early A.A.'s Spiritual Roots and Successes*, *Hope!: The Story of Geraldine D., Alina Lodge & Recovery*, *Utilizing Early A.A.'s Spiritual Roots for Recovery Today*, *The Golden Text of A.A.*, and *By the Power of God: A Guide to Early A.A. Groups & Forming Similar Groups Today.* The books have been the subject of newspaper articles, and have been reviewed in *Library Journal*, *Bookstore Journal*, *For a Change*, *The Living Church*, *Faith at Work*, *Sober Times*, *Episcopal Life*, *Recovery News*, *Ohioana Quarterly*, *The PHOENIX*, *MRA Newsletter*, and the *Saint Louis University Theology Digest*.

Dick is the father of two married sons (Ken and Don) and a grandfather. As a young man, he did a stint as a newspaper reporter. He attended the University of California, Berkeley, where he received his A.A. degree, majored in economics, and was elected to Phi Beta Kappa in his Junior year. In the United States Army, he was an Information-Education Specialist. He received his A.B. and J.D. degrees from Stanford University, and was Case Editor of the Stanford Law Review. Dick became interested in Bible study in his childhood Sunday School and was much inspired by his mother's almost daily study of Scripture. He joined, and was president of, a Community Church affiliated with the United Church of Christ. By 1972, he was studying the origins of the Bible and began traveling abroad in pursuit of that subject. In 1979, he became much involved in a Biblical research, teaching, and fellowship ministry. In his community life, he was president of a merchants' council, Chamber of Commerce, church retirement center, and homeowners' association. He served on a public district board and was active in a service club.

In 1986, he was felled by alcoholism, gave up his law practice, and began recovery as a member of Alcoholics Anonymous. In 1990, his interest in A.A.'s Christian roots was sparked by his attendance at A.A.'s International Convention in Seattle. He has traveled widely; researched at archives, and at public and seminary libraries; interviewed scholars, historians, clergy, A.A. "old-timers" and survivors; and participated in programs on A.A.'s roots.

The author owns Good Book Publishing Co. and has several works in progress. Much of his research and writing is done in collaboration with his older son, Ken, who holds B.A., B.Th., and M.A. degrees. Ken has been a lecturer in New Testament Greek at a Bible college and a lecturer in Fundamentals of Oral Communication at San Francisco State University.

Dick belongs to the American Historical Association, Maui Writers Guild, Christian Association for Psychological Studies, Alcohol and Temperance History Group, The Authors' Guild. He is available for conferences, panels, seminars, and interviews.

How to Order Dick B.'s Historical Titles on Early A.A.
Order Form

Qty.

Send: ____ *Anne Smith's Journal, 1933-1939* @ $16.95 ea. $_____

____ *By the Power of God* (early A.A. groups today) @ $16.95 ea. $_____

____ *Dr. Bob and His Library* @ $15.95 ea. $_____

____ *God and Alcoholism* ** @ $17.95 ea. $_____

____ *Good Morning!* (Quiet Time, etc.) @ $16.95 ea. $_____

____ *Making Known the Biblical History and Roots of Alcoholics Anonymous* ** @ $24.95 ea. $_____

____ *New Light on Alcoholism* (Sam Shoemaker) @ $24.95 ea. $_____

____ *The Akron Genesis of Alcoholics Anonymous* @ $17.95 ea. $_____

____ *The Books Early AAs Read for Spiritual Growth* @ $15.95 ea. $_____

____ *The Golden Text of A.A.* @ $14.95 ea. $_____

____ *The Good Book and The Big Book* (Bible roots) @ $17.95 ea. $_____

____ *The Oxford Group & Alcoholics Anonymous* @ $17.95 ea. $_____

____ *That Amazing Grace* (Clarence and Grace S.) @ $16.95 ea. $_____

____ *Turning Point* (a comprehensive history) @ $29.95 ea. $_____

____ *Utilizing Early A.A.'s Spiritual Roots ... Today* @ $14.95 ea. $_____

____ *Why Early A.A. Succeeded* @ $17.95 ea. $_____

[For 14 vol. Set, put $199.95 in "Subtotal" & $25.00 in S&H] Subtotal $_____
** **God and Alcoholism & Making Known not incl. in 14 vol. Set**
Shipping and Handling (within the U.S.)****   Shipping and Handling (S&H) $_____
        Add 10% of retail price (minimum $4.50)
**** **Please contact us for S&H charges for non-U.S. orders** Total Enclosed $_____
Name: _____ (as it appears on your credit card, if using one)

Address: _____ E-mail: _____

City: _____ State: ____ Zip: _____

CC #: _____ MC VISA AMEX DISC Exp. _____

Tel.: _____ Signature _____

Special Value. Get the Set!

If purchased separately, Dick B.'s 14 titles would normally sell for US$256.30, plus Shipping and Handling (S&H). Using this Order Form, you may purchase sets of all 14 titles for **only US$199.95 per set**, plus US$25.00 for S&H (USPS Priority Mail).

Please mail this Order Form, along with your check or money order made payable to "**Dick B.**", to: Dick B., c/o Good Book Publishing Co., P.O. Box 837, Kihei, HI 96753-0837. Please make your check or money order payable in U.S. dollars drawn on a U.S. bank.